CRY
FROM THE
MOUNTAIN

CRY FROM THE MOUNTAIN

Daniel L. Quick
with
Thomas A. Noton

World Wide

A ministry of the Billy Graham Association

1303 Hennepin Avenue.
Minneapolis, Minnesota 55403

Library of Congress Cataloging in Publication Data:

Quick, Daniel L. and Noton, Thomas A.
   Cry From The Mountain

1. Fiction   I. Title

85-052208

ISBN 0-89066-064-6

CRY FROM THE MOUNTAIN

© 1986, World Wide Publications,
Published by World Wide Publications,
1303 Hennepin Avenue, Minneapolis, Minnesota 55403

Printed in U.S.A.

Chapter One

Early morning light fanned silently across the Chugach Mountains and into the upstairs window where Cal lay awake. He had been staring at the clock for at least an hour. He watched the minute hand creep tediously toward six o'clock. The sound of the freeway traffic grew as Anchorage stirred out of a lazy Alaskan night.

Although he was excited about the float trip that lay ahead for him and his father, his ten-year-old understanding sensed a deepening problem. As he thought about it, tears welled up in his eyes. He blinked and wiped them away quickly and jerked his gaze back to the clock.

Within seconds the alarm jarred his deep thoughts and the youngster's feet hit the floor. At the same instant, his hand cut the alarm short. He grimaced at the sudden silence that enveloped the room again. Cal eyed the jumbled sheets. For a moment, he felt torn between his excitement of the float trip and a desire to crawl back under the covers and sleep away the nagging realities of life. He shook his head and his straight brown hair swirled around. It was time to forget the loneliness of his private thoughts and face a new, and better, day.

7

Cal stepped over and jerked the cord of the off-white venetian blinds and they rose with a repetitive clatter. The still morning air was filled with the scent of fireweed. He peered up into the sky. A few cirrus clouds streaked wispy, white brush strokes across the dark blue panorama. There was no sign of rain. A slight smile tugged at his mouth. "Perfect," he grunted. "It's gonna be perfect!"

As he dressed quickly, he checked himself in the mirror. Rounded cheeks reflected his boyish good looks. He hesitated in front of the mirror for a moment, lifted an eyebrow, then turned and scurried down the stairs. His untied boots clomped on the hardwood floor as he headed through the hall toward the garage. As he passed the living room, a frown pulled his smooth brow into a wrinkle. His noisy progress came to an instant halt. The shades were still drawn and he squinted, peering into the murky room. He swallowed hard.

A twisted, lumpy bundle of covers was heaped on the couch, with a pair of bare feet protruding from one end. At the other end of the tangle, a stirring revealed his dad's half-opened eyes and matted hair. The man's large hands wrestled the covers back enough for him to squint at his watch in the dim light. Then through blurry eyes, he stared over the heap at his eager son.

Cal bit his lower lip, choked back his understanding and forced a broad smile. He waved a high hand. "I'll load up the truck, Dad. Don't worry about a thing." He turned and headed out.

Before his father was able to respond, Cal was on his way to the garage. The sandy-haired man rubbed his eyes and looked at his watch again. He mumbled and tugged at the knitted afghan, finally freeing himself. He stretched, stood stiffly, and shuffled toward the bathroom. Passing the stairs, he glanced up to where his wife slept — or where he figured she was at least giving it an attempt. He sighed and shuffled on.

In the garage, Cal eased his dad's new Blazer out onto the

driveway. His feet could barely reach the brake pedal, and he had to strain to see over the steering wheel. Yet the maneuver was accomplished with little worse than a jerky start and a somewhat abrupt conclusion. His dad had initiated the ritual several weeks before, at Cal's tenth birthday. Although his father repeatedly told him he was very grown-up for his age, Cal's first few times of driving had still been near disasters. Now though, he had the feat fairly well under control. Cal jumped down and went around to release the rear tailgate latch, then hurried around the truck and headed back into the garage.

Supplies for the float trip were piled to one side of the garage. Cal spent weeks gathering items, repeatedly packing and unpacking several of the stuff bags until he was sure everything was just right. On the center post, between two garage doors, he had tacked up a long and important checklist. The list reflected his careful consideration of each item with repeated marks. Looking over the list periodically, Cal placed the bundles into the back of the four-by-four, taking pains to check off each item named. Weeks had been spent in preparation for this event as he and his father poured over outdoor magazines and camping books checked out of the school library. Although Cal's first-hand experience was limited, he had amassed a fairly extensive knowledge of what should be assembled for such an adventure. Preparation was his responsibility, and he had felt proud when his dad gave a smile of approval after checking through the assorted packages.

As he packed the Blazer, Cal stopped and eyed three large bundles heaped together. Two weeks before their scheduled trip, his father brought home those unusual packages, along with an extensive assembly manual. Within the canvas bags were countless wooden ribs and connecting rods that, according to the manual, could be compiled with a long tubular structure of canvas and rubber. Somehow, that conglomeration would transform into a sleek, two-man kayak. Though his dad warned him not to unpack their contents, Cal had spent secret moments peeking into those bags, fantasizing about the look of the craft and the excitement this float trip would bring.

Cal knelt down and stroked the sleek, varnished paddles strapped to the outside of the bundle. He ran his fingers along their length, admiring their splendid polished sheen. The boy's heart quickened at the thought of dipping them into the clear, cool arctic lake.

His wistful fantasies were jarred by the sound of his parents in the kitchen. Their words were low and muffled, but edged with that familiar sharpness. They were fighting again. He knew it wouldn't be any different. This day would be just like the others. With teeth clenched and his lip curled in frustrated anger, he snorted and grabbed another bag, dragging it to the back of the truck. Anger filled his young mind as he heaved the bundle onto the tailgate, rattling its contents in an effort to drown the kitchen sounds. Finally, he deafened himself to the voices as he pushed and poked and heaved the rest of the supplies into the back of the truck.

In the kitchen, Cal's father jabbed his fork at the half-eaten egg. He caught one edge of it and slid it back and forth, then stared at the plate for a long moment. Finally, he looked up at his wife. She had turned away to busy herself with the previous evening's dishes. He stared at the back of her head. Her auburn hair looked as though it hadn't felt the touch of a pillow and he wondered if she'd even gone to bed last night. Biting his lower lip, he searched for something to say, anything that would soothe things a bit. Nothing came to him. There was a long, uncomfortable silence.

She fumbled with the sink sprayer, rinsing one plate after the other in mechanical repetition. A deep sigh shook her slender frame and she finally broke the granite silence again. "I should be there when you tell him, Larry," she muttered. Her voice was breaking.

Larry frowned and dropped his fork in his plate. "Carolyn, come with us," he pleaded. "Just come along."

She jerked around to face him. "No!" she shouted. Her

answer ricocheted through the kitchen, echoing in Larry's ears.

She was determined not to let her husband manipulate her again. He had always been more skillful with words, and out-argued her. This time, she promised herself, she wouldn't let it happen. Turning back to the sink, she jammed the sprayer into its receptacle and stared out the kitchen window at the golden haze of sunrise. Tears formed a mist across the lower lids of her dark eyes. She blinked and droplets ran down her soft cheeks. She was a beautiful woman, and the mist of tears only enhanced her natural good looks. She swallowed. "Ten days of pretending?" she muttered. Her mouth opened and she turned to face Larry again. "I can't be out there with you for ten days." She swallowed into a cottony throat. Her eyebrows pulled to the bridge of her straight nose in a reluctant frown. "I might *really* hate you then."

Larry's lips pinched into white rage. His teeth were clenched as he spoke. "None of this is *my* idea." He pointed an accusing finger at her. *"You're* the one whose pushing for this divorce." His eyes flashed at her. "You haven't even considered the pregnancy. You're too busy flaying me with . . ."

"Me!" Carolyn shouted. Her eyes blazed. "What about Laurie?" Her voice lowered. "Your secretary wasn't my idea, mister!" Carolyn shook her head. "She was *your* idea." Her chin quivered as she stretched her smock across her stomach and looked down at the slight paunch. Her eyes moved up to glare at him. "You'd better not blame me for this either."

Her words reached across the kitchen and slapped him in the face. He flushed and grit his teeth, then caught himself and glanced toward the back door. He knew Cal could hear their shouting. He slumped, drained from all the arguing and weary of their constant verbal parrying. He rubbed his tired face and stared at the aggressive stance Carolyn had taken. She was ready for a fight and he was tired of it all. He sighed and spoke softly. "Look, Carolyn, I've been on the rack for weeks." He held up a hand in defense. "It's true, I deserved to be up there. And, I'll admit, I decided to stay on that rack because I was filled with guilt, but now I'm bloody with being sorry." Searching her glaring eyes for a glimmer of softness, he realized she was standing on the other side of an unseen icy barrier. Somewhere in the hustle and scurry of living they had lost contact and he wasn't even sure where or when. "We haven't been able to connect our thinking in months." He smirked and shook his head. "Or has it been years?" He took a deep breath and blew it out through puffed cheeks. "You've put up walls you don't even know exist."

Carolyn's mouth was drawn, her beauty marred for the moment as she scanned back through the eleven years of their marriage. She realized he had never really understood her and it was clear he never would. With jerking motions she pulled her eyes from his and covered her mouth with her hand. She finally blinked and looked back to where he was seated. "You *have* to tell Cal," she muttered. "But he's waited for this trip for a year, so do me a favor." She softened for the moment. "Wait until the last day." She stared into Larry's eyes and hesitated. "Please."

Larry grimaced and shook his head. He got up and started out to the garage.

Carolyn turned away from him to continue with the dishes. "Then I'll pick up the pieces," she whispered. She knew he hadn't heard her as the back door closed. Tears welled up again and she drew her full lips into a thin line. Her normally smooth brow wrinkled into frustrated confusion. She heard the Blazer start and she slumped forward allowing the water to run aimlessly down the drain. Then she shut the water off and wiped her hands on the towel. She hurried into the bathroom and dabbed at her eyes, attempting to cover her disturbed countenance. As much as she wished there was another way for them to get to the plane, it hadn't come about, and she needed the Blazer. A short tap on the horn hurried her along. She took one last check of her face and headed for the back door.

As the trio rode, Cal's eyes danced. He watched his dad maneuver the truck through the morning traffic. Cal noticed his mom glance around and smile at the excited look on his face. He perched his elbows on the back of the front seat and pressed as far forward as his seat belt allowed. "Hey, Mom, what ya gonna do while we're gone?"

Carolyn brushed her hand lightly through Cal's hair. "Oh, probably sleep till noon." She winked at him. "And I'll eat out a lot I suppose."

Cal searched his mother's puffy eyes. His face grew pensive. "When we get back, you'll be there to meet us, won't you?"

Carolyn glanced at Larry's undaunted profile, then back to her pleading son. She smiled and patted his cheek. "Sure, honey."

His eyes enlarged into bright ovals. "Boy, I'll bring you a real surprise! Something special from the mountains." His round face lit up with delightful hope.

Carolyn smiled her approval, but her mind really wasn't prepared for his conjured excitement. She thought more practically for the moment. "Son? Did you pack the extra socks I put out for you?"

Cal stared out at the passing traffic, then glanced at his mother as though he had just heard her. "What socks?"

She smirked. "Cal!" Her voice had that scolding tone. "They were in a brown paper bag, right next to your pack. They were clearly marked."

Cal glanced around at the pile of supplies in the back of the Blazer. "Oh, sure. I got plenty of socks."

Carolyn sighed. She became insistent. "Well, be sure you use them." She started to turn back to look out the windshield but thought better of it and continued her lecture. "And if your feet get wet, be certain to grab an extra pair of socks and put them on right away." She glanced back and raised an eyebrow. "I don't want you getting sick out there

in the middle of nowhere."

"Aw, Mom," Cal whined.

Larry didn't take his eyes off the road. "He'll be okay. I'll see to it." He slowed the truck as they neared an intersection.

Cal's hand suddenly shot forward. He pointed to a small, white arrow sign at the far side of the road. "There it is!" he shouted. "Hood Lake. It's that way!"

They turned off the main street and headed down a long row of small aircraft. At the far end of the paved parkway they could see a bright slash of gleaming water that grew into a wide expanse as they approached. As far as Cal could see, there were brightly colored float planes parked wing tip to wing tip, all around the perimeter of the lake.

Larry drove the truck along the dirt driveway that circled the water. He stopped the Blazer near the water's edge. "Here we are." He pointed out the window. "There's Glen's plane."

A sky-blue craft was docked at the end of a wooden walkway. A sandy-haired man, dressed in a red plaid coat and floppy waders, stepped off one of the floats and onto the walkway to wave as they got out of the Blazer. "Good to see you again, Larry," he called. He smiled as the two men shook hands. Glen glanced up into the sky. "Looks like everything is in your favor."

Larry cocked his head. "Looks good. Let's hope this weather holds for the next couple of weeks." He nodded toward Cal who was already pushing his head into the open door of the plane. "Uh, Glen, that's my son, Cal."

Glen leaned forward and spoke softly. "Looks like he's anxious to get going." He smiled broadly then raised his voice. "All right, let's load her up and head for the back country." He winked as Cal looked around at him.

Larry glanced back to where Carolyn leaned against the truck, silently watching the men with her excited son. The breeze ruffled her long auburn hair and she brushed it back with a quick move of her hand. She was nervous. Even at that distance, Larry detected a mistiness in her beautiful eyes. The tension of the last few weeks was evident on her face, and the urge to go to her and hold her and kiss away the hurt surged within him. He wished he could say something, or do something, but every carefully crafted phrase only sounded hollow and pathetic. He shook the disturbing thoughts and placed a hand on Cal's shoulder. "Son, your mom's waiting." He nudged the boy forward then stepped around to make his way to the opposite side of the Blazer and begin unloading the supplies.

As Cal approached, Carolyn leaned down and gathered the youngster up in her arms. He was too big to lift, but she desperately wanted to lift him and cuddle him and take him back beyond the hurt and torment, back to the good life of a baby, a loving husband, and happiness. For a long moment, she held the boy tightly against her breast. She blinked back the mist of her eyes in an effort to see and think clearly. The longer she held him, the more she realized she was near the breaking point. With concerted effort she gathered her composure and eased her grip on her son. Her slender fingers lifted his chin and she looked down into his youthful face. "Hey, partner, don't try for any world records. Okay?"

He gazed up into her lined face. A solemn look set his eyes. Even with that, the sun danced off those eyes and sparkles of excitement surfaced. He smiled. "It's gonna be great," he assured her. He gave her another quick hug, then stepped back to stare up at her. "Don't worry, Mom. You'll feel a lot better after you get some rest. You'll see."

A flash of pain swept across Carolyn's face. She hadn't wanted Cal to see what was happening inside her, yet she couldn't cover her deep feelings with superficial smiles. Somehow, the boy understood.

They exchanged a final wave as the youngster ran down to the plane to make his way into the back seat.

Carolyn watched the craft taxi out onto the lake. With a surge of power, the float plane skimmed swiftly away, cutting two white streaks across the placid lake. In a moment it lifted one float, then the other. The water calmed again as the plane rose steadily into the blue haze. She continued watching until the aircraft faded into a speck as it passed over the mountains. Her body heaved with a sigh and she slid behind the wheel of the Blazer. She realized she was facing nearly two weeks of lonely reflection and uncertain planning for the future. She started the truck and pulled around to head back home.

After nearly twenty minutes of subconscious driving, Carolyn pulled the truck into the garage and set the brake firmly. The lonely drive home was simply a prelude to the deep disturbing thoughts that were ahead of her. She felt stripped of all that was dear and precious. The sharp aching of her emotions boiled out into the open until she could contain them no longer. She slumped against the steering wheel, her head buried in her folded arms. Her shoulders shook violently with her deep sobbing. The tears flowed freely and the muddy thoughts and confusion drained out through her eyes. After sobbing heavily for several minutes, her cries waned into whimpering. She sniffed and wiped her nose. The bitter edge of despair slowly dulled and she pulled herself together. Through red, swollen eyes, she checked herself in the rearview mirror. The woman in the reflection was not the woman she'd hoped to see. Her hair was mussed and matted and her red eyes appeared as mere slits.

Finally, she slipped out of the truck and nearly staggered with spent emotions. As she made her way toward the garage door switch, a small paper sack caught her attention. It was lying on its side on the floor near the support post where Cal's gear had been stacked. She stooped down and grabbed the crumpled bag. She shook it in anger. "His socks," she muttered. Her mouth opened slightly in labored breathing. Nothing was working out right anymore. She wanted to crush the bag and tear it apart. In total frustration, she jammed it between her grasping hands and headed for the back door. She struck the garage door switch with her fist and stopped for a moment. The door rumbled down its track, sealing the musty garage against the morning light as it reached the concrete floor. Carolyn stood alone in the dark silence.

Chapter Two

The plane skimmed the high rocky ridge, working its way further into the Alaskan bush. Glen's prediction for favorable weather was holding true and the country unfolded beneath the wings of the small craft with unending panoramas of sunlit spruce and birch forests. For more than an hour the trio traveled deeper into the untracked wilderness. The general lay of the land was building to a greater altitude as they headed into a high mountainous region, flanked closely on both sides by lofty rock pinnacles.

To Cal, some of the craggy forms appeared as menacing faces with reaching arms and grasping hands that wanted to crush the small plane in their stony clutches.

Glen turned the plane up a long lofted valley. The surrounding peaks joined closer together creating a formidable barrier on each side, that narrowed the further up the valley they flew. In the back seat, Cal sat as straight as possible, stretching to see beyond the plane's cowling. He squirmed back and forth, lifting himself with his elbows on the supplies that were sandwiched in on all sides. Glen had packed the plane with the care of a master guide. It was a finely developed skill, derived from countless excursions with cargo of assorted variety. In reality, the boy had not been seated in the back, he'd been packed into it. From what he could see, the valley ahead ended abruptly at a steep rampart, leaving little room to turn the plane for a possible exit.

Larry glanced back at Cal and caught his concerned look. He reassured the boy with a good-natured smile. Larry realized that Glen knew what he was doing with the plane. When it came to bush pilots, Glen was one of the best.

They neared the end of the valley. To the right, the steep talus formation opened abruptly, revealing a long azure lake in the distance. Glen pointed. "That's it," he shouted.

Cal could barely hear him over the roar of the engine. He leaned forward and stretched his neck.

Glen eyed the ground beyond the end of the wing tip. He turned to shout to Larry again. "We'll take it down to the far end." He smiled. "There's a good place to put her in there." He banked the plane and brought it across the water for a low pass. As they neared the end of the lake, he banked steeply and circled in a smooth arc, his eyes scanning the water for any flotsam, or hidden logs or rocks. At the end of the sharp turn he pointed down toward the water. Near the shoreline, within a series of ever-expanding rings, a cow moose stood. Her long nose dripped rivulets of water as she craned it toward the intruding craft. She watched the strange sky-creature sweep overhead, then with great pumping strides, she abandoned her meal of aquatic plants and vanished into the undercover

"Lots of moose around these parts," Glen called back to Cal. "They call them the 'Ghost of the North.' One minute you see 'em , the next minute they've vanished into thin air."

Cal strained to catch another glimpse of the enormous animal, but the only evidence of her passing was the shimmering circles on the quiet water.

Glen leveled the plane for the final approach. Slowly, the plane descended. The craft's floats sliced two foamy trails across the blue water as it settled onto the glassy surface.

Within a minute he brought the plane up to a long, broad sandy beach. Such a nicely formed shore line was unusual on an arctic lake, but the prevailing winds and high rocky walls surrounding the large pool had worked together, depositing the finely ground rock bit by bit, forming what was nearly a seashore beachhead.

They deplaned and neatly stacked their supplies at the top of the beach near the edge of the scrub willow. Larry opened one of the bundles and produced a large topographical map. He carefully unfolded it and the two men discussed the intended watery passage that would take Larry and Cal from the lake, down through the canyon country, and on to their rendezvous with the plane.

Glen helped him turn the map until it was situated in alignment with the prominent landmarks in the area. He traced the river system with his finger and pointed out the route. "The outlet is at the far side of the lake." He motioned toward a sharp cut in the mountains about halfway around the body of water.

Cal and Larry looked up to squint at the place.

Glen waved beyond the rocky point. "You'll find quiet water for quite a ways, then the white water appears, and things do speed up a bit." He laughed and looked at Cal. "You'll enjoy the ride, son."

Larry studied the map carefully, taking special note of the number of feet the river dropped for each mile of travel. "Are we going to have to portage around that canyon?" He directed Glen's attention to a portion of the map where the markers of elevation curved in close to the river and nearly merged into a single line. "Right there?" He glanced at Cal. "If we do, you may have a big load to carry to the next lay in, Cal."

The boy nodded his assurances to his father. "I can make it," he said.

Glen squinted at the paper. "It's hard to say if you'll need to do any walking at that point. It all depends on the water—how high it might be running. You never can be sure. I've

seen a little creek, not much bigger than a good hop, turn into an impassable torrent by late afternoon." He lifted the map closer to his face and traced the canyon with a practiced eye. "You might want to take a good look at that stretch before you tackle it. And take the time to secure your gear. There's not many restaurants between here and the pickup point." He chuckled and handed the map to Larry. "Take a little time to check things out." He looked at Cal. "That's one of the first things a boy should know about the wilderness." He winked at the youngster as he turned toward the plane.

Larry agreed with the bush pilot. "Cal understands. I think he'll do just fine. He listens and learns fast."

The men shook hands at the water's edge and Glen turned away and nudged the plane out into the lake with a push of his boot. He waded out until the water came up just past his knees, then climbed up on the float.

Larry called to him, "We'll see you in ten days at Caribou Lake."

Glen waved. "Caribou Lake. Ten," he shouted back. He waved again and slipped behind the controls, starting the engine. He stretched his arm and pointed his thumb up, then swung the plane around sharply, sending a cool spray into the faces of the pair. In a few moments the plane was far down the lake. It lifted off and climbed toward the mountaintops. Glen rocked the wings in a farewell wave.

Cal waved both arms. "See ya, Glen!" he shouted. His voice bounced back from across the water as the plane's engine quieted to a whisper in the distance. They watched the shrinking craft top the ridge and fade out of sight. Only then did Cal notice the silence. Like a creeping thing, stillness edged its way from its hiding place far back in the dark spruce forests. It slipped in from all sides, deepening as it advanced, until it covered the lake and all of the mountains like a heavy quilt.

"Well," Larry said, "it's too late to turn back now." He nudged the boy's shoulder. "Just you and me, Sport." It sounded so final. Larry noticed Cal's frozen look as he stared out to where the plane had disappeared. He nudged the boy once again. "Guess it's time we put that kayak together." Cal's face lit up. Larry acted as though he didn't notice. "Think you can give me a hand with that?"

Cal grinned. "I guess I can find the time," he joked.

For the next hour they studied the instructions and compared lengths of the wooden ribbing, trying to find just the right component to fit into just the right locations. To Cal's delight, the craft slowly took on the skeletal outline of its final form. Once slipped into its fabric shell, the sleek blue vessel seemed to come to life.

Cal stepped back to look at her. Larry put his arm around the boy. "Let's load her up," he said. They loaded their supplies and pushed the two-man kayak out into the water.

The tranquil lake mirrored the craft as it slid over the glassy surface. Cal was in the forward position, while Larry took the back where he could control the rudder. He pressed on the left pedal and the kayak swung in a gentle curve that took it out toward the center of the lake. He dipped his oar into the water, first one side then the other, in smooth rhythmic strokes.

Cal tried to match his father's alternating movements, but couldn't maintain the rhythm. His oar clacked against his father's, sending a spray of water across the back of the boat and into Larry's face.

"Come on, Cal!" Larry barked. "Put the oar in a little deeper. And slow it down. The front man always follows the rhythm of the one in the rear." Larry set up the stroking pattern again. "Let's go, son. Left. Right. Left. Right." He smiled. "That's it."

Cal's mouth broke into a wide grin as his strokes fell into proper order. The kayak surged forward smoothly.

"Now you've got it. You don't have to work hard at it. We just have to work together. That's what counts."

A light breeze ruffled the arctic lake. Glistening patterns and lacy streaks formed on its surface, then subsided and reformed again in new regions. Cal watched the shimmering designs as the boat traversed the water. It was a welcome moment for the boy. A true wilderness encounter was all new for Cal. This was far more profound than the vicarious adventures he experienced in the books and magazines he'd studied. The dark water passing beneath the kayak, the pleasing aroma of the pines, even the awesome silence that permeated the trackless miles of tundra and forest, all reverberated with adventures he had only read about.

The kayak slipped across the lake and entered a wide lagoon that meandered for several hundred yards then narrowed slowly as it formed the tributary that would carry them toward Caribou Lake. Along the banks were fresh cuttings of the resident beaver, and near the end of the lagoon, rising from the tranquil water in a great mound of mud and sticks, was the animal's lodge. A streak of bright water snaked a path of ripples on the surface near the lodge and marked the trail of the industrious animal. The beaver eyed the invaders from a distance then ducked beneath the surface, sending out his warning with a slap of his flat tail. From deep within the watery lagoon a grayling rose from its deep shadowed refuge, paused, shot to the surface, snatched a newly hatched mosquito in its jaws, then darted back to the mossy branches beneath the beaver lodge. The disturbance caught Larry's attention and he directed the kayak toward the grassy bank.

The pair spent the rest of the warm afternoon pursuing the delights of the angler. The bank near the beaver lodge stood clear of any brush and offered a superb platform for fly fishing. Beavers had cut trenches that criss-crossed the bottom of the lagoon, providing the grayling with a natural habitat of shadowed hiding places. With Larry's help, Cal caught on to the knack of moving the long, slender rod back and forth until he could place the fly into the most tempting locations.

Cal whipped the rod tip back and then forward, allowing a little more line each time.

"Out a little further, son," Larry instructed. "Work those

dark areas. That's where the lunkers hang out," he called.

Cal swished the line again, letting the feathered Black Gnat settle gently on the water. He flipped the end of his rod, and the lure twitched as it floated on the surface. In the next instant, the water beneath the fly swelled, then broke in a silvery spray as the fish grabbed the fly and darted for the bottom, Cal's lure firmly planted in the side of its mouth. "Hey, Dad," Cal shouted.

Larry dropped the supplies he was working with and looked up.

Cal jerked back on the slender rod. "I've got one!" He could feel the heavy tugging at the other end of the line as the big grayling sliced through the water and headed for the branches near the base of the beaver lodge.

Larry hurried over to Cal's side. "That's it, son, keep the rod tip up. Don't let him get into those branches or he'll break the line for sure."

Cal stepped back from the bank, forcing the fish to turn toward the open lagoon. The line sang through the water, first one way, then the other. Cal kept backing away from the fish until his shoulders were pressed against a thick hedge of alders that were growing a fair distance from the water line. Larry turned and saw what was happening. If he hadn't called to the boy, Cal might have continued right back into the undercover.

"Hold it, son." He waved his hands and motioned Cal forward, back toward the water. "Don't try to drag him out! Stand in one place and let the tension of your rod do the work."

Somewhere between Larry's shouts and Cal's jumping up and down, the big fish managed to end up on the bank. Cal ran to the spot and pounced on his prize. Grasping the shiny grayling in his tight fists, he held it high in the air for his father to see. "Wow! Look at him, Dad! He's a beauty."

Larry smiled. "Nice going, son. He's a dandy all right."

Late evening brought the lingering light of the arctic

summer sky, casting a gentle glow across the surrounding mountains into the simple campsite. Larry stretched a plastic tarp between some trees to form a snug, protected sleeping area. Cal had cut tender green branches from some of the younger trees and placed them under the tarp, weaving them into a soft springy mat. The fire pit was a few yards in front of the covered area. Larry dragged some logs that worked nicely as benches into place near the fire. From somewhere back on the lake, the lonely lament of a loon floated through the spruce boughs and filled the camp with its melody. Cal listened to the call as he watched the day's catch sizzle in the pan, their rich aroma drifting up with the swirling smoke. He leaned down close to the fire and loosened the crisp grayling with a spatula.

Larry eyed his son as he worked over the meal. It was good to let the boy have the responsibility for cooking the fish. The fact was, he wasn't sure he could have done much better, and after all, Cal had caught the biggest one that day. He watched Cal place one of the fish onto his waiting plate, then serve himself a generous portion. Larry smiled at his son and nodded an invitation for the boy to dig in. He waited eagerly as Cal carefully savored the first steaming bite.

"Well?" Larry chided. "Before I dig in, I want to know if they're worth eating."

Cal merely smiled and dug in for a second larger bite. His eyebrows raised and his lips smacked. He left little doubt that the meal was a smashing success.

Larry followed Cal's lead and eagerly joined in the feasting. "Ummmm," Larry licked the salty flavor from his lips. "Now that's what I call fine chow!"

Cal beamed. He took another large bite, then looked back up at his father. "Ever float this river before, Dad?"

Larry finished another bite and wiped his mouth with the back of his hand. "Nope. But I did a survey for a mining company near this area. That was several years ago and we used helicopters to get in and out of the country." He paused and looked around at the gray outline of the forest. He squinted into the growing evening. "Just not the same that way."

Cal raised his eyebrows and looked up into the late evening. A haze was settling over the camp. "Is there any gold around here?"

Larry shrugged. "Could be. Used to be in some parts of these hills, but that was years ago." He noted the boy's growing interest. "Of course, there's always the chance of someone finding a new vein." He wiped his mouth again. "There's a bunch of country yet untouched in Alaska. I'm sure there are lots of secrets in these mountains."

Cal placed his empty plate to one side and picked up a long stick. He really didn't notice how deep the darkness was growing, but focused on the fire. He jabbed the stick into the glowing coals, sending up a shower of sparks that floated into the charcoal sky. They swirled in the smoke like a cluster of tiny red stars. He watched the miniature embers wink out one by one. "Wish Mom could be here." He smiled. "I wish she could have seen me catch that first grayling. She'd a loved it." His grin slowly faded and he poked the stick at the logs again. His jabbing produced a fresh shower of sparks. His voice was low and sullen. "Mom's been kinda edgy lately."

Larry pretended to bypass the remark as he scraped his plate with the side of his fork, cleaning up the last tasty morsels. "You know, your mom's not much for camping," he muttered.

For a long moment the boy was silent as he stared into the flickering fire, listening to the crackle of the burning wood. "I know I messed up with my grades and that could'a upset her." He twisted the stick in the embers, then glanced up at his dad. "Tell her I'll bring my grades up, will you?"

Larry cleared his throat and adjusted his position on the log. "Son, it isn't your fault she's upset. She's going through some very rough times now, what with the new baby coming and all."

Cal tapped his stick on the side of a burning log. He set

the point firmly against it and rolled it over. His eyes lifted and met his father's watchful gaze. He swallowed. "Do you love mom?" he asked. His voice was husky—suddenly mature.

Larry's brow wrinkled. The honesty of Cal's question was inescapable. His pulse quickened and perspiration formed tiny beads on his forehead. His voice was too high-pitched. "Well, sure I do." He stood and stretched as though the conversation would end, but he added, "It's just that sometimes married couples have problems."

"I don't understand," Cal countered. He was genuinely puzzled.

Larry realized there would be no easy way to dodge Cal's inquiries. "Son, I, ah," he hesitated. Finally the bewildered man put ambiguity aside to face the problem directly. He leaned against a rough tree. He wasn't at all sure this would be the right time or place. He thought about Carolyn's request, but he couldn't wait until the last day of the trip. What had to be said, had to be said, and the timing was important. He sighed and turned back to look across the fire into Cal's pleading eyes. He took a deep breath and began. "Maybe you are old enough to handle this." He gathered his thoughts and cleared his throat. "Your mother and I have talked it over, and she wants a *divorce*." He attempted to sound matter-of-fact.

To Cal, his father's final word hung on the evening air. The boy's eyes flashed a mixture of pain and anger. "But you said you loved her." When his father didn't respond, he jabbed the stick into the fire with vehemence, then turned his narrow eyes up to stare at his father.

Larry looked at the odd expression on Cal's face. They stared for a long moment.

Cal's mouth twisted and he snorted before he snapped, "Who's Laurie?" His chin quivered and he hated the thought of crying now. "Who's Laurie?" he shouted again.

The question was like a raging bull in Larry's mind, and he felt the sharp pain of a goring horn go through him. For a long moment the two were stalemated. The man felt powerless against his son's determined pursuit. He swallowed, nearly choking. "S-she's a friend, f-from the office," he stammered.

"What's she done to upset Mom?"

Larry tried. "Son, you won't understand, but she and I went out together a couple of times." His lips were very dry. "Understand?"

Cal understood. His teeth clenched and he jammed the stick into the fire. His eyes snapped up to glare at his father. "Why?" he screamed. "Is she prettier than Mom?" He saw the instant flush on his father's face. With mounting anger he jumped to his feet, whirled and ran into the gray darkness surrounding the campsite.

"Cal!" Larry shouted. Although deeply concerned, he knew he had to let the boy take a walk. Larry grit his teeth and his jaw muscles flexed. He turned to the tree and slammed his fist into it. His knuckles cracked. He was angry with himself for allowing it to happen. The day had been so perfect. He hadn't meant it to come out this way at all. The timing he'd thought was so precious was all wrong.

Cal stood near the river looking into the dark swirls and eddies that meandered by. He wiped his eyes with a sleeve, determined not to show his tears. Stooping, he picked up a smooth, flat stone from the sand and flung it across the water. It skipped several times then disappeared into the fading light. He could hear his dad in the campsite, preparing everything for a secure evening. The movement stopped and a shiver ran through Cal's body as a chilly gust of night air ruffled his hair. His young mind was tormented with a strange mixture of anger and shame. He was angry at the way his parents were being torn apart, and ashamed of the way he had reacted to his father. Sighing, he turned back to look at the glowing embers in the distance. With a grimace, Cal slowly shuffled back to the camp.

When he approached, he could see his dad was already

in his sleeping bag. A lantern was burning near the head of their bedrolls. Cal stepped around the back side of the tarp and slipped his boots off. He quickly climbed into his bag, keeping his back toward his dad all the time. He pulled the folds around his face and stared out into the dark trees. The mournful sound of an old hoot-owl echoing through the forest was soon answered by another, further away. The night air had chilled quickly and he could just detect his breath in the light of the lantern. He heard his dad stir.

Larrry reached over and gently placed his hand on Cal's shoulder. He squeezed it.

Cal was glad his dad was close by. The big hand felt good.

Chapter Three

Morning dawned with a gray and sullen sky. Clouds moved in from the southwest, carried on a chilly breeze. The air was damp, and the surrounding mountaintops were obscured by whiffs of fog that streaked down from their summits like hoary locks of hair, ruffled in the wind.

Cal sat near the fire, prodding his oatmeal with the back of his spoon. He scooped up a small portion and placed it on the end of his tongue. Because he had dallied so long, the sticky substance had cooled and hardened into tasteless lumps. He frowned as he squeezed the stuff between his tongue and palate, then turned his bowl over and scooped the remaining glob into the smoldering ashes.

Larry sat across the campfire and eyed his son. He didn't want to get anything stirred up, so he allowed Cal his silent meditation. But now it was time to break camp and prepare to move on. Larry stood. "Well, let's get at it," he said. He didn't look the boy in the eyes, but merely began to work as though nothing was strained between them.

Within an hour, the camp was secured and the kayak packed for travel. Larry helped Cal into his life jacket. "That'll do ya," he said. He made an effort to be lighthearted but the youngster didn't respond. Larry sighed and helped the boy into the front seat, then stepped into the kayak with one foot and pushed off with the other. He shoved the craft out into the cold, gray water. The slender kayak teetered slightly as he situated himself in the rear compartment. He centered his grip on his oar and stroked slowly. His lips parted in a slight grin as he watched Cal pick up the rhythm. They moved from the lagoon into the deep indigo river. The current meandered back and forth as it pushed toward the mountainous country.

They traveled downstream for several miles. Sometimes they used the oars; other times the kayak drifted with the current. In any case, Cal had mastered the stroking cadence and they moved down the tributary at a leisurely pace.

The lower mountain slopes interrupted their downward plunge in a series of rolling knobs that flanked the river banks on both sides. A dense forest of birch, cottonwood and Sitka spruce guarded the river's banks and intermingled throughout the area. At times the river would undercut the bank, causing some trees to lean far out over the water, their branches bobbing in the moving current. They kept the kayak well away from possible root snares and "sweepers." Glen had warned Larry about the potential danger of a swirling current taking the kayak into overhanging branches that could sweep everything off the water's surface into the tangle of underwater limbs and roots. Though the current was slow, it was strong, and the pair of adventurers had to make their course changes well in advance.

About noon, Larry broke the silent drifting. "Looks like we've done seven or eight miles," he called. He stared at the back of Cal's unmoving head, sighed and looked down at the blue water. The movement had been fairly constant and the tranquil current afforded them a relaxed ride. They stopped rowing for a bit and let the current bear them along. Larry reached down between his knees, lifting his day-pack into his lap to check the map. He pulled the map out and looked over the line of their route. The valley ahead of them narrowed and entered a restricted passage. Looking over the edge of the map, he eyed Cal. The boy was peering aimlessly downstream in unfocused melancholy.

Larry glanced back at the map. It showed him they would soon encounter a series of sharp bends, some of which nearly turned back on themselves, then quickly reversed direction. The area was vast. Most of the mountains in the region were yet unnamed, but one of the map's elevations caught his eye. Somewhat separate from the other peaks drawn there, its base sloped nearly to the edge of the river. According to the elevation rings, its topmost pinnacles pierced the sky a thousand feet above any surrounding summits. It appeared to have several summits forming a horseshoe amphitheater above a high bowl-shaped valley carved into the rim of the mountain. Larry looked at the small print, just to the side of the crescent of pinnacles. "Mystery Mountain," he muttered. His eyes narrowed as he studied the pyramid-shaped landmark.

"Dad!" Cal shouted. His voice was edged with anxiety and it jerked Larry's attention.

The man's eyes snapped up.

Cal pointed ahead of the kayak. Just fifty yards downstream a steep rocky outcropping loomed in craggy danger on the right side of the river. It forced the gurgling water to make an abrupt left. The water boiled up against the rocks and a standing wave stood two or three feet higher than the surrounding water.

Larry barely had time to react. He jammed his foot against the left pedal and stuffed the map down between his legs.

Cal's brow furrowed deeply and his eyes darted back to his dad, then forward to the direction they were forced to go.

Larry grabbed his oar, striking deep into the churning water. Cal followed his father's lead. The sleek kayak veered toward the left bank, away from the craggy rock formation. The current picked up and instantly they reached the sharp corner. Both of them stroked frantically. Together, they swung in close to the left bank, while a forceful watery hand pulled the craft around the blind turn. As they rounded the rocky shoreline, Larry's heart sank. On the inside corner of the hairpin bend, an enormous sweeper protruded far out over the water, directly in their path. The leaning spruce reached nearly half way across the river. Its entire length created a tangle of broken branches and twisted driftwood.

"Pull hard, son!" Larry shouted above the rumbling torrent. Cal's paddle dug into the icy water. Larry matched his strokes, dipping his own oar deeper with each thrust. The muscles in his arms bulged and the paddle quivered under the force of his stroke. The kayak turned toward the far end of the tree. There was no time to reverse the craft and try to fight directly into the current. With each stroke the boat surged across the flow, yet the kayak looked as though she'd be taken into a treacherous tangle, nearly side on. The oars fought the surging current. Seconds split into fragments of desperation. With a last deep plunge of his paddle, Larry pulled with all his strength. The nose of the kayak slipped under the upturned tip of the menacing sweeper. Branches scraped along the side and top of the boat with a squeaky, scraping chatter. Larry watched Cal duck under the reaching branches, then pulled his paddle in close to the side of the kayak to keep it away from the boughs. Through the foliage he could see that Cal had passed beyond the branches and was preparing to set his paddle for another stroke. Leaning as far forward as possible, Larry felt the branches scrape along his head and back. The boat slowed and listed precariously. For what seemed like a long suspended moment, the craft stopped. It was momentarily dead in the water. Then it slipped and pivoted around the end of the tree. They were free. Within seconds the kayak again drifted peacefully in the current.

Cal twisted around to look back at his dad. Numerous evergreen needles and small broken twigs perched at odd angles all the way from his matted hair to his waist. The boy watched as the man mocked his son's gawking stare.

Cal burst into a broad grin. "Wow!" he shouted. "We made it!"

Larry's eyebrows raised and he checked from side to side, then grinned at Cal. "Yup, it appears we did." The man took a quick look at the sides of the kayak. It had come out unscathed. He smiled at Cal again. "You all right, son?"

Cal opened his hands, palms up. "Sure, not even a scratch." The boy was excited and overly animated. He really hadn't realized the full impact of their experience, nor the hidden danger they'd just passed.

After glancing over his shoulder at the receding branches, Larry turned back toward Cal and shook his head. "That was a close one," he wheezed. "Too close for me. I think I'm ready for some good old *terra firma*. Let's put in for awhile."

A short way down river the water shallowed near the left bank, forming a quiet backwater. Larry guided the kayak into the eddy, toward a portion of the bank that sloped gently into the water. They jumped out and pulled the craft well up onto the bank.

Larry stretched for a moment, pressing his hands against the small of this back and swaying in an attempt to loosen his knotted muscles. "Feels good to give your legs and arms a stretch now and then." He winked at Cal.

Cal nodded. "My arms feel weak." He smiled warmly. "I'm sure glad we didn't get wet." He smirked. "I never did find those extra socks Mom said she put out for me."

Larry grunted a slight disapproval, but didn't press it. Instead, he changed the subject. "Hey, let's check the map and see what's up ahead." He retrieved the folded paper that had been hastily crumpled on the floor of the kayak and placed the map against his chest, smoothing the wrinkles with his hands. "I'm sorry about that scrape back there. I guess I got too involved with the map." He smiled at the boy and reached out to ruffle his hair.

Cal shrugged and rubbed his head in an attempt to straighten the tangled mop. "That's okay. It was kind'a exciting."

Larry raised his eyebrows in less than total agreement. He sat down next to the boat, placed the open map across his knees, and glanced at his son. "Come and sit over here. Let's look at it together."

Sitting down beside his dad, Cal watched as the features were pointed out.

Larry's mouth widened. "Look at this mountain. It's called Mystery Mountain." He motioned up over his shoulder. "It's right up there behind us. Right now we're sitting at the base of it." He fingered the spot on the map. "Right about here." Sucking in his lower lip, he raised his eyebrows. "It really looks interesting up on this side, near those top pinnacles." He turned to gaze up at the actual thing then turned to look into Cal's inquisitive face with an easy smile. "Why don't we give up dodging sweepers for the rest of the day and do some exploring? It looks like the clouds are lifting some and we can camp right here for the night. We got plenty of time." He grinned at the boy. "What do you say?"

Cal looked up toward the rock summit, his eyes dancing with sudden excitement. "You mean we can go all the way up to the top?"

Larry gazed up again and frowned a bit. He sucked the side of his cheek in and nibbled at it. Then he bumped Cal's shoulder. "We may not go all the way up, but I bet we could reach that high bench, just below those rock walls." Placing the map on Cal's legs, he pointed at the high valley outlined on the map. "See here. There are several streams that feed out of that bench. Gold quartz comes out of strata like that."

Cal's eyes widened. "Really?"

"Yup. Who knows, you might find a little color in one of those streams."

"Color?" Cal frowned.

"Gold," Larry said. "Maybe even a nugget. Wouldn't that be a great addition to your rock collection?" He grinned. "You never know. We might get lucky."

Scrambling to his feet, Cal stared up at the mountain.

"Yeah! I'm gonna find a big gold nugget." His grin broadened and his voice rose with excitement. "I'm gonna find a real big gold nugget and I'm gonna give it to Mom." His eyebrows shot up and his eyes widened. "Hey, maybe I'll even have it put on a ring for her."

Larry nodded and smiled at the boy. "She'd like that, son. At least we can give it a good try."

For the next few hours, Cal and Larry worked their way up the steep slopes toward the towering pinnacles. Once they had climbed above the timber line they followed the tops of hogback ridges. These crests meandered up the wide face of the mountain, offering an open, sometimes steep pathway to the top. They avoided the wide brushy areas of alder that blanketed much of the upper slopes, covering the side of the mountain in enormous textured patches of dark green. A few times they were forced to inch along a narrow finger of one of the brushy areas. The alders were tall and dominant, woven so closely together that they were nearly impossible to penetrate. The snarled limbs grew close, in aligned and twisted patterns reaching up to twenty feet. Their dark-green leaves formed a thick canopy that blocked out the light and suppressed the air within the thickets until it was a stale, humid mass.

By mid-afternoon they crested a high sloping bench that continued to lead them further up the mountain. "Now the angle isn't so steep," Larry called back to Cal. The tall grass of the hogbacks gave way to a lush carpet of tundra, profuse with a perpetual variety of wild flowers.

Cal liked the feel of it. Each step was met with a spongy response from the ground cover which reminded the youngster of walking on a thickly padded carpet.

At times the slope leveled into a small flat terrace, wide enough to pitch a tent. They merely used those areas as rest stops.

During one of those periods Larry stopped to rub his burning calves. He eyed Cal to see if the boy was all right.

Cal was bent forward with hands on his knees. He gasped

for breath. "Boy, I-I can, ah, hardly breathe." His lungs heaved in an attempt to catch up with the pace.

Larry looked over the edge of the flat rock. Far below, the shiny ribbon of river wound through the hill country and into a dark canyon.

After a short rest, the pair of adventurers angled around the slope toward a wide depression that appeared to cut its way down from the same upper bench they had spotted on the map. A crystalline brook danced down the open draw, spilling from rocky steps into deep sandy pools, repeating the process numerous times on its plunge to the deep canyon.

Larry eased around a large boulder and dipped his hand into the icy water to lift the refreshing liquid to his lips. It was sweet and fresh. With a tired sigh, he slipped his day-pack from his aching shoulders.

Cal flopped down against his pack and closed his eyes. He took in the thin air with deep, heaving breaths.

Larry looked at his son. A slight grin tugged at his thin lips. He bent down and snaked his hand into his day-pack. His hand finally touched cool metal and he withdrew two flat charcoal-gray wash pans.

"Hey, Sport! Here ya go." He waited until Cal opened his eyes, then tossed one of the pans to him. "This looks like a good place to see if we can find any of that gold." He waved Cal over to the brook.

Cal got up with sudden enthusiasm. He watched his dad scoop his pan into the water, bringing up a fist-sized mound of multicolored sand.

Larry looked at the youngster. "Pick up a little sand, then kind'a swish it around in the pan so that the water can carry away the lighter material." He demonstrated the technique as he talked. "Gold is heavy stuff. It will settle to the bottom as you wash the sand away. If you're careful, you can find even a piece as small as a speck of dust."

Cal watched his dad work the first pan of sand. Then he shoved his pan into the brook to scoop up the stuff. The frigid water made his fingers tingle as he forced the pan into the sand. He withdrew it and watched the sparkling sand swirl around the flat container. He worked the sand around, allowing some to spill over the edge with the water. When the water ran out and there was still sand left in the pan, Cal dipped back into the surface of the cool brook and got more water with which to swirl the sand. Somehow the slow plodding of panning for gold was less than exciting for the boy. The adventurous high country called to him for more expressions, more movement, more excitement. Besides, Cal didn't want to look for *dust*. There were nuggets to be found out there. He continued to pan, but slowly eased away from the patient concentration of his father. Cal sloshed the last bits of material from another pan-full, then headed up the knoll that flanked the small brook. "I'm going to try upstream," he called back to his dad.

Larry was busily panning and thought he had a nugget. He picked it out of the pan and smirked. "Nothing," he muttered. He glanced up to see where Cal was. The man frowned as he watched the boy crest a knoll and disappear. "Hey, Cal!" His call didn't bring Cal's head popping over the edge of the knoll, so he quickly ran his finger through the remaining grains of fine silt in the bottom of his pan. He searched for any sparkle. Nothing. He rinsed the container and headed up the hill after his son.

Up ahead, Cal trotted across a gentle incline, now and then jumping on top of a tundra hummock, then leaping toward the next one. As he reached the crown of the knoll, he was arrested. His eyes widened and his jaw hung limp in gaping astonishment.

Perched against the steep hillside, right at the base of the final rocky pinnacles, was a conglomeration of old weather-beaten buildings. The dilapidated structures were scattered across the hillside, set at odd angles to each other in a jumbled pattern that drew his attention higher up the mountain. At the uppermost point of the talus were several larger buildings, straddled against the base of the rock walls.

Stretching across these highest structures was the lofted arc of an old trestle, its gray weathered timbers streaked brownish red from its rusting tracks. Broken planking, crumpled tin, and rusting machinery was strewn throughout the complex. Cal froze in captured wonder. He was awe-struck at the sight of the ramshackle structures that formed a ghostly edifice. His mouth gaped open. "Wow!" For a moment he stood transfixed, the gaping windows and doors peering down at him in lifeless vigil. He whirled around to start down the knoll but ran into a man's grasping arms. He screamed, "Dad!"

"Son," Larry said. He saw the wild look in Cal's eyes. "Son?" He shook the boy. "Are you okay?"

Cal relaxed and swallowed. "You scared me. I-I thought you were somebody else."

Larry snickered. "There's nobody else within fifty miles of here." He shook his head in mild humor.

Cal jerked around to look back out across the rocky area. "Yeah, well take a look at that." His hand swept across the picture of old buildings. The panorama was awesome.

Larry's gaze slowly gathered in the breathtaking kaleidoscope. "It's an old mining camp." His mouth opened slightly as his eyes traced the progression of weathered buildings. "And a big one too."

Cal's eyebrows raised in delightful enthusiasm. "It's a whole town."

They stood their ground for a moment, then Larry dropped his pack on the large flat rock. He nudged Cal's shoulder. "What do you say, we go check it out?"

"Yeah!"

They started up the easy slope, Cal close behind his father. As they approached the outlying buildings the entire network of wood and rusted tin expanded to an even greater magnitude. The wind off the higher rock buttress whined through the cables that stretched from the lower buildings, all the way to the top of the pinnacles. Here and there, across these high rocky perches, were the scars of old deserted mining shafts, their dark mouths laced with rotting timbers.

An overgrown pathway snaked its way up the hillside and led them into the heart of the buildings. As they rounded the first structure, their way was blocked by a large rotting sign. It had been conspicuously placed in the main trail. They stopped and studied the weather-checked words.

Cal read the sign. "Stay out!" He squinted. "Ken-Kencordia Mining Company." He looked up the trail. "Hey, Dad, look up on the hill." He pointed. "Somebody must live here." He grinned, "I thought you said there wasn't anybody within fifty miles."

Larry looked up to where Cal directed. Far up the hillside, well above most of the other buildings, set just to the right of the main mining structures, a one-room cabin stood on a small rounded butte. A blackened stovepipe protruded from its rusty tin roof, and from the stack a small but distinguishable swatch of dark smoke streaked across the gray sky.

Larry edged forward a few steps. He couldn't see any sign of life around the tiny building but the smoke was undeniable proof that someone was around. He cupped his hands to his mouth and shouted toward the cabin. "Hello there! Hello, cabin!" His voice bounced between the wooden buildings and the rocky walls. Nothing moved or responded. He studied the cabin carefully. On its porch he could just make out the outline of a rocking chair, draped with some sort of animal skin. He was sure that anyone in the area could have heard his call, yet the entire complex remained ghostly quiet.

Larry whispered. "There's somebody here all right."

His hushed voice made Cal uneasy. The boy glanced up through anxious eyes.

Larry licked his lips and stepped back. He cast a searching gaze at the small building. He looked at Cal. "We can only . . ." He stopped. A deep-throated growl caught his attention. The hair on the back of his neck tingled and he reached out and pushed Cal back. Larry's eyes darted for a sight of the animal.

An imposing-looking shepherd inched his way into the center of the trail behind them and his growl deepened.

Larry and Cal whirled around to face the animal. Cal's eyes widened and his mouth gaped as he pushed back behind his father.

The dog's shoulders were squared toward the pair. His hackles bristled and he growled again. The rumbling in his throat continued as his lip curled to bare his teeth.

The animal stood in the path the two had just crossed. Larry spoke with soothing authority. "Easy, big fella." He pulled Cal close to him, then backed off the trail and began a wide skirt around the animal. "It's okay, boy. We're not going to hurt anything." He kept his grip on Cal's shoulders and pulled him along in protective shielding.

Standing his ground, the dog slowly turned with their movements. As they reached the trail below the warning sign, Larry pushed Cal to the down-hill side, keeping himself between the boy and the angered dog. He stared at the animal's penetrating eyes as they moved away from the area, around the old buildings and back toward the rocky knoll.

When they passed around the last building, Larry looked back up the trail. The dog was gone. He vanished as quickly as he had appeared. The man's eyes scanned the buildings for a sign of the animal but all was quiet as before. "Whew!" He glanced at Cal.

The boy finally spoke. His voice was timid. "I wonder if somebody left him up there. He looked like he may be part wolf."

"I don't think he was part wolf." Larry was contemplative. He rubbed his stubbled chin, then sighed. "He didn't look hungry to me. I suspect some people don't want to be bothered by anyone. After meeting their dog, I'm inclined to respect their wishes." He patted Cal's shoulder. "We better move on."

Chapter Four

The two climbers struggled through the maze of branches. Finally, Larry edged his way up the last few steps toward a tilted slab of stone that protruded out of the river, forming a steep overhang nearly fifty feet above the swirling water. The top broke into a large, flat platform. He glanced back to see how Cal was doing, then scooted himself onto the level perch. He turned back to lie flat on his stomach and stretch down to catch Cal's wrist. As he helped the boy up toward the crown of the huge stone, his firm grip on Cal's arm reassured the youngster. Larry held on until Cal was near the center of the platform, then grinned at the boy. "Hey, pardner, I'm knocked out. How about you?"

Cal wheezed and sat up. "Me too." He looked over the panorama. "But it sure was worth it. We can see for miles."

From their high lookout, they could see a mile or more down the canyon. Larry lifted his binoculars and studied the river as it channeled through the narrow gorge below.

Cal watched his dad thoughtfully. He reached out and broke off a stock of fireweed. Along this section of the river, the fireweed had begun its annual magenta display. Cal examined the cluster of flowers. Then, in an attempt to discourage a persistent mosquito, he swished the stock back and forth in front of his face. He inspected the top of the stone he sat on and ran his finger along the tiny fractures created by eons of heat and cold whose network formed tiny footholds for the plants.

Larry lowered the binoculars. "The water doesn't look too bad." Lifting them again he continued to glass the rapids as far into the canyon as possible. "Looks like there might be an exciting point or two along the way." He glanced at Cal. "But most of all, just clear sailing."

Cal swatted blindly at the persistent whining wings of the insect bent on using him for lunch. He leaned back and focused on the end of his nose in an attempt to locate the mosquito. A small blur darted across his line of vision, then there was a slight tickle as the mosquito touched his forehead. A quick slap stopped the annoyance, permanently. Cal lowered his hand and studied the tiny bit of crumpled legs and wings, then with a puff of breath, sent the miniature carcass tumbling on the breeze. He lifted the stock of flowers to his nose and sampled its soft scent, thinking his mother would like the fragrance. He stared at the cluster.

Larry lowered the glasses and looked at the boy. "Heavy thoughts, huh?"

Cal sniffed the fireweed again and sighed. His eyes fixed on the distant river below. "Oh, I was just wondering . . ." The youngster hesitated for a moment.

Adjusting his position, Larry looked curiously at Cal. Finally he broke the silence. "Now so am I." He smiled easily. "Care to spill it?"

Cal squinted and bit at the inside of his lower lip, then looked his father straight in the eyes. "I was thinking about you and Mom. And I was thinking about the baby that's coming." He rested his elbows on his knees and placed his chin in the cup of his hands. "Well, what's the point of having a baby brother or sister if you're not going to live together anymore?"

Larry raised his eyebrows, twisted his head and sighed.

He wanted to attack this delicate subject with as much warmth and wisdom as possible, so he cleared his throat and thought a long moment. "Cal," he began, "our divorce doesn't mean you're going to be left without the joy of a baby brother or sister." He reached out and placed his hand on the boy's shoulder. "We're going to do what's best for you." He patted the boy. "Both of us will."

Cal glanced up at his father then nodded. "What's best for me is having both of my parents." He looked down to the granite earth. "Not choosing which one I want to live with." The feeling hung heavy.

Wiping his frown away, Larry attempted to lighten the moment. "Hey," he nudged the boy's shoulder, "we're supposed to be having fun. How about it?"

Cal nodded and smiled politely.

"Good. Now, why don't we gear up and take on that canyon? It looks like the water is at a safe level, and I'm in the mood for some white water excitement. Are you game?" He slapped Cal's back.

The boy easily forgot the insurmountable problem. His head swiveled to look toward the river again. "White water!" His voice rose with excitement. "Let's go!"

It took just minutes to make their way back down the rock and along the river to the waiting kayak. Larry helped Cal with his life jacket then double-checked the tightness of the chin strap on the boy's helmet. A final check of his own equipment and a quick confirmation that their supplies were securely tucked inside the nose and tail of the boat, and they were ready to go.

Their spirits were high as they slid the craft into the water. In some cases, the rocky river banks formed vertical walls on each side that kept the forest away from the river's edge and lessened the chance of further encounters with sweepers. The current moved in great meandering swirls of quiet, forceful water, bearing the craft swiftly along its back. Cal quickly picked up the cadence of Larry's rowing pattern while Larry pressed alternately on the pedals to check the rudder system. The wires that fed back along each side of the craft and hooked to the rudder cross-member, slipped effortlessly in their guides, swishing the rudder back and forth.

"Keep a sharp lookout for hidden rocks, Cal," Larry instructed. "Call out if you see any. When we get to the rapids, keep your balance centered."

Cal nodded, and started chanting a song in time with their rowing motions. "Row, row, row your boat, gently down the stream."

Larry grinned and joined in with the melody. "Merrily, merrily, merrily, merrily, life is but a dream." He laughed out loud and the sound of it echoed down the canyon. To him, life had no finer hour. The crystal-clear fragrance of mountain air, the rush of the powerful river, and laughter with his son — these, for Larry, had captured the essence of life.

They guided the kayak into the center of the current. As they neared the first bend, the river narrowed somewhat and the speed of the flow increased. A light chop formed on the river's surface. Larry kept the boat centered in the current and they rounded the corner smoothly. A stone's throw ahead, the river dropped in a series of small choppy waves, then leveled for one hundred feet before dropping again. Each downward step of the river brought new turbulence to the water, agitating the waves into small whitecaps. The kayak slipped through the first set of waves, bobbing and rocking slightly. A noticeable increase in speed caused Cal's face to beam with exhilaration.

The boy turned back to look at his dad. "Yahoo!" he hooted over the increasing roar of the surging water. Larry grinned at the boy, then cautioned him. "Keep your weight centered." He didn't know if Cal heard him over the increasing volume of the thundering rapids.

As the kayak sped over the next step and shot down the sloping staircase of churning waves, water lapped up onto the boat's cover, dousing the pair with cold spray. The wooden ribs and joints of the craft squeaked as the kayak's frame twisted slightly in the turbulent water. Larry held the craft steady with a backward push on his oar, taking care to keep the nose of the kayak headed directly into the rough water.

They passed the furthest point Larry had been able to see with his binoculars. Now he kept a watchful eye on the water ahead, trying to read its fickle character. At the next bend the river turned sharply to the right, dropping several feet and gaining momentum. The push of turbulence against the back of the kayak erased the effectiveness of the rudder, and forced Larry to control the boat's direction solely by the action of his oar. The boat shot through the white water, picking up speed. Larry back-paddled in an attempt to slow their pace.

Cal stopped rowing and hung on to his oar with a white-knuckled grip. As the boat cleared one set of rapids, it glided onto a brief swirl of quieter water.

Larry sat as high in the craft as he could, watching the water down canyon. Ahead, the rock walls that skirted the river suddenly closed in, forcing the current to plunge through a tight restriction. The water seemed to explode as it crashed through the narrow rock chute. Larry could see large standing waves tossing white spray high into the air. "This is gonna be some strong stuff!" he shouted. He realized Cal couldn't hear him. He craned his neck to see beyond the chute. There was more angry white water and the rocky banks offered little chance for escape. He didn't hesitate, but shoved hard against the left foot pedal. "Pull hard, Cal!" he shouted. "Head for the bank!"

Cal's eyes were wide as he stared at the on-rushing torrent. His grip tightened on the oar but his arms remained frozen.

Larry shouted as loudly as he could. "Cal!"

The shout broke the spell and the boy struck the oar hard against the current. The kayak turned slowly toward the left bank but continued slipping toward the narrow chute. The craft was catapulted from a high swirl into a deep depression, surrounded with high walls of raging water. They were jerked out of that thunderous pool into an explosion of ragged torrent. The kayak shot into the rough water at an angle and tilted dangerously. Larry pulled back with his oar, forcing the craft to swing around again. It was clearly too late for any escape to the safety of the bank. They would either pass through the narrows, or be crushed under tons of water smashing their tiny craft against the large boulders.

Now out of control, the kayak plunged into the huge waves. For a moment the front of the craft disappeared beneath the water then broke clear again as the boat streaked on into the narrow passage. Chilling water poured into Cal's lap, soaking him to his feet. The kayak raised up to the top of a standing wave, then nosed down the other side. As water crashed in on all sides, it flooded the inside compartment.

Larry pulled his oar against the raging waves in an attempt to keep the boat straight. The kayak shuddered with the impact of the crashing water, then listed to the right and rolled.

The shock of cold stunned Cal. He was instantly enveloped by the blue-green water. The current pulled him down, deep under its churning surface. He could feel an endless shower of bubbles streaming by his face. His only other sensation was the numbing frigid blanket of water all around him, sweeping him deep within its folds. Far above his head he saw a lone shadow. He reached up toward the dark object but his movements seemed slow and laborious. He was sure the object was the kayak. He had to reach the craft and his dad. Although he stretched his arm high above his head, the speeding current seemed to take him further away. The passing boulders along the banks were a blur of swiftly moving objects. He tried again, struggling with all his might. Grasping for the surface, his life vest was snagged by his dad's powerful hand. Suddenly he was yanked up, and his head was out of the water. He gasped as his face was bathed in a blast of light. Feeling the kayak bump up against him, he instinctively reached for it. At the same time he felt his dad give him a hard push toward the floundering craft.

Larry shouted above the roar. "Stay with the boat." He too hung on tightly. "Hang on, here comes some rough stuff."

The smashing force of a wave knocked Cal's hands free from the slippery skin of the boat. He flailed in an attempt to grab the craft again but the next wave flipped the kayak far from his reach. He lost sight of his father and panicked. For a moment, all he could see was frothy water mounting up on all sides. Then he was lifted high on the back of another huge wave. As he crested the top, he looked for any trace of his dad. Further out in the river, he could see the gray upturned side of the kayak as it was being swept through the rapids. His father was nowhere in sight. Cal shouted, "Dad!" His cries were muffled by the roar of the water. Again, and again, his shouts were lost in the spray and mounting thunderous rush of white water. The mighty current pulled him down into another trough then tossed him high on the back of a white crest. All he could see of the boat was an occasional flash of gray.

Instinctively, he fought for the rocky shore, digging at the water. Rocks along the bank swept by in a dizzying blur. Cal struggled to the shore, his body numbed by the bone-chilling water. Blindly he kept reaching forward and grasping at the water. When his fingers finally brushed against a limb, his hand grabbed it and locked on. The waterlogged fir tree had been grounded on some rocks next to the shore. As he caught the limb, the current of rushing water attempted to strip him from its safety, pulling at his legs and swinging him around violently. In a moment, his body was flung against the tree. His fingers slipped on the polished branch and his hold was broken. He scraped along the side of the tree, his hands desperately searching for something to grab. As he neared the end of the tree he grasped a cluster of branches. This time his grip was sure. As his legs swung

around the end of the tree, he felt his knees touch the rocky bottom. Pulling his feet beneath himself, he pushed toward safety. Half stumbling, half crawling, he fell up onto the bank and with the little strength left, forced his body upright to stagger up the embankment.

As he reached a large boulder, he whirled and looked out at the raging water. Down river, just rounding a rocky point, he caught a glimpse of his father's blue life vest and white helmet. Larry was far out in the current, trailing the kayak by several yards. In the next instant he and the boat disappeared around the point. Cal started running along the shoreline. "Dad!" His rage flashed against the powerful waters. "Oh, God! No!" The boy felt helpless. "Dad!" he screamed. "Dad!" He stumbled up to a jagged outcropping of rocks, then saw his father and the kayak plunge through another turbulent chute before vanishing into the narrow canyon. "Oh, God, help me," Cal shouted. "Dad!" The boy scrambled over the moss-covered stones in a frantic attempt to follow the river down. The rock-strewn shoreline was wet and irregular. Cal's feet twisted and sent him sprawling onto the rounded boulders. He hurt his knees, but gathered himself and continued on.

As the canyon narrowed, the shoreline ended abruptly at a long vertical wall. Cal hurried up the steep bank that rose sharply. Grasping at roots, he climbed above the impasse and skirted along its upper edge. The top of the wall was covered with a mass of tangled brush and dead-fall timber. Pushing his way through the branches, he jumped from one toppled tree to the next. As he reached the end of the cliff, he peered down at the river and moved his head from side to side so he could see through the maze of branches. The shoreline below had widened as the river swung to the right. Against the bank, in a pool near the base of the cliff, he caught sight of a dark slash of blue. "Dad!" he shouted. With nimble moves, he ducked under the limbs and slid down the steep slope, tunneling through the twisted network of branches. As he reached the bottom, he burst out of the thick brush and stumbled onto the river's bank. A few yards to his side he saw his father's limp form. His head and arms were draped over the rough river stones, his torso and legs floating in the water.

Cal plunged into the pool, and grabbed hold of the blue life jacket, pulling with all his strength. It took everything he had, but he was able to slide his father up onto a gravel plateau and out of the chilling water. Blood streaked down from his father's forehead and Cal stared at the limp body, which appeared lifeless. He swallowed hard. Bending down and rolling his father to one side, he leaned close to listen for the sound of his breath. His hand covered his other ear to block out the sound of the raging river. He squinted and listened, barely feeling the slow, shallow breathing against his ear.

Cal sat up and gently shook his father's shoulder. "Dad, are you okay?" There was no response. The boy looked at the blood oozing from a cut near the edge of his father's helmet. The man's puffy face appeared to be turning light blue. In panic, Cal shook his father violently. "Daddy!" he screamed. When there was no response, Cal whined, "Oh, Daddy . . " Tears streaked down his fearful face as he bent forward and gathered his father in his arms. He struggled and pulled the man's head up into his lap to remove the helmet. Desperate fear mounted and swept through him. He moaned. "Oh, Daddy, what am I going to do?"

He laid his cheek against his father's forehead, without noticing that the blood flow had slowed a bit. He lifted his head and searched up and down the riverbank for any sign of help. "Daddy," he whimpered again, then wiped his eyes with the side of his hand to clear his tear-blurred vision. The dark canyon and forest were stark and desolate. Except for the endless roar of crashing water, there was no movement. Cold jagged walls of the canyon looked down on the boy with stony disregard. Above the high cliffs, Mystery Mountain loomed in the distance, its rock spires draped in gray clouds. Cal stared at the great landmark. A sudden light flashed in his mind. *The mine.* The thought jarred him. "Someone lives at the mine," he remembered.

Cal laid his father's head on the gravel bank, then got up and yanked his life vest off, wrapping it into a smooth pillow to place under his dad's head. The boy's jerky breathing came in surges as he tried to choke back his convulsive sobs. He bit at his lower lip and gently brushed his fingertips across Larry's cheek. "I'll be back," he choked. Turning, he quickly scrambled up the brush-tangled embankment and headed back up river toward Mystery Mountain.

He crested one boulder and then ran up a sparse path toward another. He bounded along, ducking the overgrowth and leaping over small rocks in his way.

The minutes seemed like hours as he hurried up stream. As he stumbled up the last tundra bluff that crested near the entrance to the mining complex, Cal's lungs heaved painfully. His shirt was torn and soaked with perspiration. Exhausted, he stumbled toward the rickety wooden sheds that stood at the perimeter of the ghostly camp.

"Help!" he shouted. His voice was harsh and breathy. He coughed and tried to shout louder. "Somebody help!" He forced his aching legs to climb the steep path that led to the base of the towering trestle. "Please! Somebody. My Dad's hurt bad!" His eyes swept the hillside, searching for any sign of aid. The mountain wind moaned through the weathered lumber of the deserted buildings, and a gaping door groaned on its rusty hinges. Cal staggered up the hillside, following the path that zigzagged through the scattered relics, mounting ever higher toward the solitary cabin. As he rounded one of the rotting structures, he stopped suddenly. Directly in his pathway stood the large, gray dog. The animal eyed the frightened boy curiously. Cal held his breath, his voice caught in fear. He edged away from the animal, one tenuous step, then another. He swallowed and felt a desperate scream swell in his throat, but it refused expression. In final confusion, he whirled around and plunged back down the pathway. Instantly he collided with the belly of a tall, solitary figure. Cal screamed. Large weathered hands grabbed his shoulders and shook him.

"What's wrong with you, boy?" The voice was gruff and deep.

Cal looked up through tear-filled eyes. He blinked away the blur and stared up into the face of an old man towering over him. The sun in back of the man seemed to produce an aura of light around him, his long gray hair ruffled by the wind.

Chapter Five

By late afternoon the winds had shifted, blowing the foggy mist from the rock summits of Mystery Mountain. The arctic sky was a blaze of contrasting colors as the sun drifted low in the northwest, inflaming the cobalt sky with florid rays. The weathered buildings of the dilapidated mine stretched out their long irregular shadows across the tundra slopes, giving the scene an eerie complexion.

Even though the old man hastily constructed a litter from small spruce trees, and with Cal's help dragged the heavy load up a hidden mining trail, it still took all day to transport Larry up the side of the mountain to the cabin. At times, the path narrowed so that Cal could do little more than follow along behind and help guide the trailing skids, while the grizzled old man singlehandedly hoisted Larry up the stony pathway. Cal could only guess at the man's age. He looked ancient to the lad, mysterious and aloof. In spite of his leathery skin and speckled gray beard, he was obviously a man of great strength, but puzzling character. His eyes were squinted and drawn at the corners, piercing in their stare, and yet at the same time they were surrounded with the wrinkled evidences of laughter. He wore a soiled, broad-rimmed hat planted squarely on his head. His fleece-lined coat was somewhat tattered at the sleeves and his double-thick canvas pants were supported by wide red suspenders that buttoned at the waist. Over his shoulder hung a handmade leather sling attached to a *Model 70 Winchester.* Its stock had a dull finish which bore the marks from many years of faithful service. Cal noted that the old man always favored the weapon, switching it from side to side on occasions when overhanging limbs or rocks offered any chance of contact.

Cal's comments had been met, for the most part, with silence or guttural grunts. The old man saw conversation as an unnecessary part of the day's events. Cal tried again. "You never told me your name, mister." He watched the back of the man's head. When there was no response, he thought he'd try a more direct approach. "My name's Cal. What's yours?"

The big man stopped short. The skid stopped right in front of Cal and he nearly tripped. "Jonathan," the man grunted. "My name's Jonathan." He turned back and looked as though he'd begin to pull again, but hesitated and looked over his shoulder at Cal. "Don't care too much for useless conversation." Staring at the boy, a slight grin tugged at his parched lips. "Pleased to meet you." He turned back to the task and pulled.

Jonathan had surrendered to the boy's urgings, but he wasn't set to give out much more than his name. He had chosen to live in the wilderness. This pair was invading his private domain. He didn't like it, but he wasn't unkind.

When they reached the cabin, Larry was still unconscious. Inside Jonathan lifted the limp man onto the old bed, a large brass relic held over from days past when the mining camp was bursting with activity. The old man dressed the wound on Larry's head, cleaning it, then wrapping it with a long section of torn sheet.

Cal watched with interest as the old man worked his gnarled fingers down his father's legs, checking for further injuries. Larry's left shin was badly bruised but appeared to be unbroken. The boy wondered about the confident way in which Jonathan carried out the examination. "Were you a doctor?"

The old man grunted. He seemed to be somewhat annoyed that the boy would place the question in the past tense. He shook his large head and smirked. "Nope," he snickered. "But you don't work in a mining camp all your life without learnin' somethin'." He checked the unconscious man and determined that he'd done all he could before looking at Cal. "Come on, boy. We gotta get you out'a those wet clothes." They pulled and tugged at the soaked clothing.

When Cal was stripped and in one of Jonathan's large shirts, the big man whistled at the dog. "Come on, Jake." He pushed out the door without a word to Cal.

Cal stood near the bed and studied the room. The day's last rays of sunlight bathed the single room through a hazy four-paned window just to the right of the door. Although its glass was frosted with years of neglect, the sunlight illuminated the pane with a rosy glow. Curiously, this window and two others on the side walls were framed with lacy curtains, somewhat dingy with age, but still reflecting a decidedly feminine influence.

Feeling a slight chill, Cal stepped over to the cast-iron wood-stove in the center of the room, slightly warm from tiny embers glowing on the lower grate. He warmed his hands over the black monstrosity, the blackened rust-streaked pipe reaching up through the rafters to the open ceiling. A rustic wooden table near the stove was accompanied by three high-backed chairs. Sliding a chair over near the stove, Cal sat while his curious glances moved around the walls. At several points, snowshoes, tools and clusters of steel traps were attached. Cal got up, eased over to the far wall to take a closer look, and inched his way down to the end of the room. There, he brushed his hand over an antique, foot-operated organ. Its irregular keyboard dipped now and then with stuck keys, giving the appearance that the instrument had clung to the imprint of some long-past itinerant musician. Cal wiped his finger over the dusty organ. The particles tickled his nose until he thought he'd sneeze, but he held his nostrils closed and tried to prevent the occurrence. The feeling left and he looked over to his sleeping father. He was glad he hadn't sneezed and wakened his dad, but he was concerned about the fact that he was still unconscious.

Cal shrugged and turned toward the back wall. There he saw a series of shelves, reaching from the floor, all the way to the slanted ceiling. Most of the shelves were lined with canned goods. The old man had stored up a supply adequate for several months. Cal picked up one of the cans. "Beans," he muttered. His nose wrinkled. He put the can back and looked around. Near the center of the wall, a large section was set aside for a most interesting collection of scattered paraphernalia. The lower shelves were interrupted by a small rolltop desk. Framing the desk on both sides and on two upper shelves, was a hodgepodge of magazines, books and papers, and just to one side of the desk, on one of the lower shelves was an old radio.

Immediately, Cal was captivated with the instrument. He studied the relic with its cloudy amber dial and ornately designed pointer. Carefully, he stroked its dusty surface, slipping his fingers down the front louvers until they rested on the black tuning knob. Slowly he turned the knob back and forth. The pointer swept across the numbers. He wondered what programs could be heard on such an instrument. He thought they would be very old and mysterious ones.

Cal's eyes shifted from the radio to where he spotted a large, heavily-textured, black photo album. He slid the book from the shelf and lifted the front cover. The scrapbook was filled with an endless collection of faded black and white pictures, browning with age, dating back to the days when the mine was active. At one time it *had* been filled with life and excitement. Slowly he turned the pages, studying the photos with intense interest. There were pictures of the buildings, new and sturdy, filled with men bent on making their fortunes in the gold fields. There were shots of machines, big machines and long barrel-shaped tumblers where the ore was beaten and crushed. And more men, posed in smiling youthfulness, their picks and shovels in hand, somewhere deep within the tunnels and shafts of Mystery Mountain. There were family photos too. He paused and studied a vertical snapshot. The picture was placed in the center of one of the pages, held in place at the corners by small black triangular sleeves. The photo stood alone on the page, though it was no larger than the others crowded on similar pages. In the picture, stood a youngish man with a beautiful young woman on one side of him and a boy, about Cal's age, on the other. "Jonathan," Cal muttered. His forehead pulled into a frown. "I wonder where *they* are."

The latch snapped and the door opened suddenly. Jonathan and the dog stepped from the porch into the room.

Cal jerked and slammed the book shut. A cloud of dust puffed up between himself and the glare of the old man. The boy quickly slid the album back into its place on the shelf.

Jonathan looked at the boy, then glanced at the album. He said nothing and shut the door behind him. With deliberate strides, he went to the table and threw a carcass on it.

Cal winced and stared at the skinless animal. He had never seen anything like it. Its red muscles were covered with whitish streaks that ended near the joints as stringy tendons. He stretched his neck and peered at the creature, plainly seeing the animal's ribs just under thinly layered membrane. Its legs were long and skinny and its thin neck ended abruptly where the head had been severed. Cal's young mind raced, trying to assign an identity to the thing. He thought it was about the size of a house cat. The thought jolted him and he felt a shudder crawl over his spine. Still wincing, he glanced at Jonathan. "What's that?" His face drew into a sneer as he looked back at the naked carcass.

Jonathan didn't look up. "Rabbit," the old man muttered. He unfolded his jackknife and proceeded with the task of dismembering the carcass into pan-size chunks.

Cal pondered the unlikely answer. He knew rabbits were round and furry and lovable, nothing at all like the lean, naked creature stretched out on the rough surface of the table. But he accepted it as fact. "Did you shoot it?"

Jonathan snorted and smirked at the naive boy. He snapped the animal's hind quarters off at the waist then looked up at Cal again. "Nah." He nodded toward the dog. "Old Jake there barked real friendly like, and the critter just hopped right up to me, then it jumped right out of its skin and into my bag." A quick thrust of his knife neatly separated the two hind legs. He didn't turn his head, but shifted his eyes to see the boy's expression.

Cal swallowed hard. His mouth twitched as he watched the old man finish sectioning the rabbit.

Jonathan grabbed a fresh-split chunk of wood and pushed it into the glowing coals of the firebox. He placed a large cast-iron frying pan on top of the stove. The log began to crackle. A large scoop of grease melted quickly in the hot pan and the seasoned portions of rabbit were added. Soon the room filled with a savory aroma.

Jake padded across the floor and curled up in front of the organ. He eyed the proceedings from under heavy brows, now and then lifting his head in anticipation.

Jonathan looked at the hungry dog. "Don't worry, Jake," he said. His voice was soft and gentle as he talked to his old companion. "I've got a couple of pieces set aside just for you."

Jake swished his tail, then laid his muzzle across his paws, keeping a watchful eye on the boy.

Cal stared at the big dog with reservation. "Does your dog bite?"

"Only if I tell him to."

Cal inched over to where he could look into the frying

pan. "He looked pretty mean yesterday when my dad and me came up the mountain."

After testing each piece of meat with the tip of his fork, Jonathan turned them over and dusted them lightly with salt. He got out another pan for heating a vegetable, then went to the shelves to select one of the cans.

Cal watched him and hoped he wouldn't pick beans. "Do you think he might have bitten us then?"

Jonathan selected a can and went to the cupboard for an opener. As he worked, he muttered, "Old Jake wasn't being mean yesterday. He was just trying to get you guys to go back and read that sign you ignored."

Somehow, to Cal, the big shepherd didn't seem so ferocious now that he was curled up on the cabin floor. The boy turned his attention to the bed. His dad was sleeping peacefully. Almost absently, he said, "He's sure been asleep a long time." His eyes misted a bit.

Jonathan didn't look up from his work. "Best thing," he muttered. He removed the crisp, golden chunks from the sizzling pan. "His head's probably pounding."

Cal grimaced, then thought it best he let his father rest. He glanced up at Jonathan, then his eyes swept around the room. He wanted to allay the fear inside, so he pushed for a change of thought. "Have you lived up here a long time?"

Jonathan shoved a plate across the table and motioned for Cal to take his place there. The old man followed the plate with a knive and fork tossed onto the dish. The clatter disturbed Jake. Jonathan stopped and stood tall. His head was up above the glow of light and he looked foreboding. "You wanna talk, or you wanna eat?"

Cal was hungry. He grinned up at the towering man. His eyebrows raised. "Eat," he ventured.

The evening darkness enveloped Mystery Mountain in its velvety cloak. The early August days had grown noticeably shorter and the evening stars reappeared after many weeks of absence during the brief nights of arctic twilight. A waning

moon rose steadily in the east, casting its silvery light on the pearly mountain tops.

Inside, the cabin was dark except for the moon's soft glow entering through the side window. Cal was curled up near the brass bed, on the folded quilt Jonathan had given him as a mat to help soften the harshness of the wood floor. A green woolen army blanket provided the top cover and his folded coat became a pillow. Jonathan rummaged up a folding cot for himself and situated it over near the small desk. For the last hour he had been snoring peacefully.

Cal rolled his eyes and listened to the rhythmic rumblings of Jonathan's heavy breathing. His dad continued his restless sleep, mumbling now and then as he stirred on the bed. Cal scooted up on his elbow and looked at the sleeping silhouette. He whispered, "Dad," then squinted, looking for any reaction.

The man uttered a muffled groan but made no other response.

Cal reached up to adjust his father's covers then scooted back under his blanket. Although it worried him that his dad was still unconscious, the old man had told Cal that it was to be expected in the wake of such an injury. He had reassured Cal that his father would be fine if given a day or so.

Across the darkened floor, Cal could barely make out Jake's form. The dog was curled up under the old man's cot, his nose resting on his forelegs. The pale reflection of moonlight formed a glint in the animal's eyes. He was watching the boy. They stared at each other across the darkened cabin. Cal had always wanted a dog of his own, but somehow it had never worked out. He pursed his lips and softly kissed the air. Jake lifted his head at the sound and wagged his tail. Cal smiled, then settled his head on his coat. His eyes searched the shadowy forms of stored items suspended between the overhead rafters. He wondered how many years the building had stood on the steep slopes and how long the old man had lived among the shadowy buildings.

From somewhere outside, Cal heard the hooting of an owl. He listened as the night bird repeated its echoing call through the spruce forest below the mining camp and on through the lower slopes, far down the sides of Mystery Mountain.

Closing his eyes, Cal drifted off. A flash of his mother's face streaked across his mind as twilight sleep closed in on him. "Help," he whispered. He didn't know how to pray, but he knew his parents needed an intervening force. Sleep quieted his restless mind.

Chapter Six

Morning light dawned bright and clear. Jonathan was up puttering around well before the sun had touched the upper pinnacles. The old man was used to an early start, much earlier, he was sure, than any city kid. He'd play the good host for a while, and let the boy sleep an hour or two, then he'd roust him out for a Sunday breakfast. He slipped quietly across the cabin to the bed and checked on Larry. The man's color was good and his breathing seemed normal. Jonathan was sure he would be up by afternoon. Although he had hoped that the man would have regained consciousness during the night, he'd seen things like this with mining injuries, and sleep was the best medicine. He'd give it until noon to see what happened with the man.

He went out and carefully latched the door after himself, then headed down the trail toward the old milling building. Jake tagged close behind. The short tufts of mountain grass glistened with moisture, and he paused along the way to admire a patch of tiny forget-me-nots hovering near the trail like a spray of petite blue stars, lightly dusted with morning dew. He loved this time of day. The mountain winds were usually stilled and the awaking world seemed to vibrate with new color and fresh smells. This was a time when a man could bounce his ideas around clearly, and distinctly consider life without the muddled distractions brought on by the stir of mid-day activities. Besides, with all the bewildering recent events, he felt unsettled and perplexed. He needed some time to back away and sort things out.

As he neared the main complex he turned down a side path that veered sharply to the left and headed toward a large shed, set on a cindered flat about two-hundred feet below the cabin. In front of the wooden structure stood the remnant of a small water tower. The holding tank had long since toppled from its timbered support and lay next to the shed in rust-streaked ruins. In front of the entrance were two ribbons of steel track, all but obscured by the windblown soil. They arched in a gentle curve away from the shed, skirting along the hillside and eventually crossing the wooden trestle that bridged the upper buildings before joining the hillside again on the far side of the mine. All along the sides of the shed were twisted piles of pipe and crumpled tin, gathered over the years by the old man. All were organized in categories of size and stages of decay. The shed's rough-sawn walls were bleached gray by many long arctic summers. Its tin corrugated roof sagged noticeably at one end, and in fact had given way at one point, forming a large gaping hole.

All in all, there was nothing about the exterior of the shed to identify it as more noteworthy than any other odd-shaped building in the area. Yet, as Jonathan approached the building's entrance, his steps slowed. At the threshold, he paused and slipped his hat from his head, then slowly continued on into the structure. Jake sat near the tracks and watched the old man disappear inside.

At one time it had been a tool shed and repair shop. And indeed, Jonathan continued to make it his headquarters for various projects and repair jobs. At the left end of the room, was a veritable heap of discarded oil drums, sheaves and boiler parts. Boxes of threaded pipe fittings were stacked along the wall. Scattered across the floor were coils of copper tubing, scrap iron, and various jars and coffee cans, filled with an endless collection of nuts, bolts and fasteners of every size. The torn section of corrugated roof arched over the near end of the room, flooding the area with streams of daylight. Through the years, pelting rain and snow had found its way through this opening, causing the rusting treasures to stain the floor boards deep auburn.

Along the back wall, opposite the doorway, was a long workbench. This too was covered with boxes of spare parts and tools. Its surface was worn smooth by years of active use. At the end of the bench, suspended from a ceiling beam, was a chain windlass which hung nearly to the floor in long heavy loops that often swayed rhythmically when the wind rattled the building. The links would tinkle together like a giant wind chime.

But the right side of the room gave the shed its unique flavor. Jonathan had carefully cleared this end of any left-over mining equipment, and had swept the floor clear of rubble. A wide slatted high-back seat had been placed near the center of the area, situated to face the end wall. Against this wall was a long bench, once used in the camp's dining hall. Near the center of the bench, resting on a white doily, was a large, leather-bound Bible. Attached firmly to the wall above was a wooden cross, fashioned from two sections of weathered four-by-fours. The light from the nearest end of the shed streamed down from the torn section of roofing and touched the cross in a diagonal swath, giving the entire setting a most hallowed appearance. In fact, the overall effect of the room was quite stunning, in spite of the contrasting assortment scattered around the rest of the room. The wall with the cross and the bench with the Bible always arrested Jonathan's attention. He stopped and stared at the hallowed site which for the old man had become his chapel.

Taking his place in the slatted chair, he brushed his fingers through his gray hair in an attempt to make sure that his appearance was proper. For a long moment he sat quietly, listening to the silence of the morning. He stared at the cracks in the floor. Finally, he looked up to the cross. His lips moved slightly and his audible words barely invaded the silence. Slowly, his voice grew bolder. "Well, Lord." He paused and took a deep breath, then let it out with a sigh. "I sure didn't choose the company. Can't honestly say I like what you're doing." He shook his head. "Too many memories laid to rest. No need in stirrin' 'em up." He lowered his eyes and watched his fingers fidget with the rim of his hat. "I remember too much, Lord. When Edna was still with me." He paused and swallowed hard. "And you know the boy being here reminds me too much of young Ethan." He looked back up to the cross. His brow was creased with the bittersweet memories of former times. They'd been carefully tucked away. "It's been me and you and Jake for so long. And all that talk the boy's doin'. You know how that grates on my nerves. I just don't know what you're after, bringin' these fellas up here like this."

Cal had dressed quietly, checked his father and slipped out the cabin door. He had heard Jonathan get up, and had listened intently to his footsteps as he headed down the path, away from the cabin. The urge to learn more about the old man and his mysterious mine proved much stronger than any temptation to linger and enjoy the comfort afforded by the warm blanket.

Gazing around at the mountainside from the rickety porch, Cal watched the sun's golden spectacle as it bathed the broken buildings in a warm, rosy glow. He sensed the presence of the dog. Forgetting the shining splendor, he turned to stare at the inquisitive animal. "Where've you been?"

Jake raised his head and watched the boy with growing interest.

Cal eyed the dog carefully, then stopped and picked up a short piece of dry root. He held it out at arm's length and nodded with a smile. Jake's tail twitched slightly. With a

quick thrust, Cal threw the root up the side of the slope. Instantly, Jake bounded after the tumbling stick. Gathering it up in his mouth, he turned and looked back.

"Come on!" Cal called, his face beaming with excitement. He patted his thighs. "Bring it here."

Jake trotted down the hill and dutifully dropped the root at Cal's feet. For a moment they looked deep into each other's eyes. The dog watching expectantly, but Cal was still a little unsure. Slowly he reached out and offered the back of his fingers. Jake sniffed and swished his big tail. He touched Cal's fingers lightly at first, then nudged his nose deep into the palm of the boy's hand. His tail wagged in great flopping waves.

"Good boy. Good dog!" Cal said. He stroked Jake's muzzle. "Where's your master this morning?" He patted the dog's head, then bent down and picked up the root, flinging it as far across the tundra as he could. At the very first movement of Cal's arm, Jake was already off and running, looking back over his shoulder for an indication of the root's trajectory. Cal trotted up the hill after him. All fear was now lost in the excitement of the game. The process was repeated until the pair moved well up the side of the slope, near the base of the rock walls. Breathless and laughing, Cal dropped to his knees and threw his arms around the dog's ruffled neck. His thick coat felt good and he buried his face in the long fur. Cal's new-found affection was readily accepted. The boyish enthusiasm quickened memories in the heart of the old dog — memories of long ago and another youth, and other games played on the knolls and gullies of Mystery Mountain.

In the cabin, Larry's eyelids fluttered. He blinked and squinted trying to clear his blurred vision. Gazing up at the criss-crossed pattern above him, the cabin's rafters made little sense to his unfocused mind. He was filled with a bewildering parade of dreamy images of Carolyn and Cal, and of water; cold, swirling water and enveloping whirlpools of crashing waves. Then came the distant sound of laughter.

He shook his pounding head. He couldn't figure out whether he heard laughter or crying. It was laughter. In fact, it was Cal's laughter he heard. He snapped his eyes open, then closed them tightly again. Carolyn was crying. He saw the hurt etched across her face. "I'm so sorry," he muttered. A dog barked.

Larry jerked and sat up. The abruptness increased the throbbing in his head and the room tumbled around. He grasped the corner of the brass bed to steady himself. As the spinning settled, he gazed around the cabin. Nothing made sense. Everything looked strange as though out of some novel he'd read. Raising his shaking hand to his bandaged forehead, he frowned and stared at the cast-iron stove. He felt sick to his stomach.

The dog barked again. And still came the sound of Cal's laughter from somewhere outside. Larry pulled himself to his feet and limped over to the door. As he pulled it open, the room was flooded with sunlight and he shielded his eyes, leaning his shoulder against the door's frame. As he adjusted to the brightness he scanned the buildings scattered across the hillside and suddenly recognized where he was. Cal's happy shrieking caught his attention again. He saw the boy romping with a dog on the side of the hill.

"Cal!" His voice resounded across the hillside, catching the boy's attention as it echoed back from the base of the rocky pinnacles.

Cal jerked up. His laughter ceased. "Dad!" he shouted. He left Jake and scrambled quickly down the rolling slope and onto the path toward the rickety porch. "Dad, you're awake!" He lunged at his father's waist and hugged him tightly. "Are you okay?"

Larry pulled the boy close. "I'm a little banged up, but I think I'm going to make it." He winced as Cal hugged him. "Easy, son, I'm sore."

Cal stepped back. "How's your leg?"

"Oh, sore, but I'm walking." He glanced around the complex. "Cal, how did you get me up here?"

"You were knocked out, so I had to come up here and get Jonathan to help me."

Larry frowned. "Who is Jonathan?"

Sunday breakfast consisted of fried mush sprinkled with brown sugar, followed by canned peaches. During the meal, Cal related the ordeal of pulling his dad out of the water and how Jonathan had brought him up to the cabin, doctored him and generally taken matters well in hand.

The grizzled old man preferred to remain silent, during most of the meal, nodding when necessary and commenting no more than absolutely required. Now that Larry was awake, the encroachment into his private world seemed even more pronounced. He figured he could endure the chatter for a day or two, then maybe with luck things would get back to normal.

As soon as the meal was finished, Jonathan pulled his pocket watch out to check the time. He held the instrument at the far extreme of his reach, wrinkling his brow as he tried to decipher its message. With a satisfied grunt, he slipped the watch back into his pocket and turned toward the old battery-operated radio. He reached behind the relic and uncoiled a bundle of red and white wires that ended with two large clips. Muttering, he pulled the wires down the face of the bookshelf and onto the floor. Then he slid a large truck battery out from under the corner of the desk and proceeded to run the wires over to its terminals.

Larry and Cal watched with growing curiosity as the old man attached the clips to the battery. Neither of the guests asked any questions. They'd already discovered it best to wait and watch. At last, Larry ventured a question that seemed innocent enough. "How far is it to the nearest telephone?" As soon as he spoke it sounded silly to him.

Jonathan lifted an eyebrow and glanced back at the man as he got up off his knees. "Humph!" he grunted, then turned back toward the radio.

"We're going to have to locate the kayak. I'm kind'a

wondering what we're up against."

Jonathan wiped his nose. "Don't think you'll be goin' nowhere." He didn't look up, but clicked one of the radio's switches. "Least not for a day or two."

The room filled with the crackle and hiss of static. Jonathan slowly turned the main tuning knob, tilting his head back as far as possible in an attempt to bring the dial into clear focus. "I see somebody's been messin' with the dial." He glanced at Cal, then looked at the old radio again.

Cal tried to bypass the insinuation. "I can find the boat," he exclaimed.

Jonathan screwed up his face in disgust. "No job for a kid. You'd be in over your ears in five minutes out there."

Larry glanced over to his son and caught a flash of disappointment. He winked at Cal. "This *kid* saved my life."

Cal smiled.

"I'll find your stuff tomorrow morning," Jonathan said. The statement carried the sound of finality. The conversation was over.

The radio's crackle gave way to the voice of an announcer. The old man smiled with satisfaction, then he stepped back and pulled his chair over near the shelf.

"Now it's Sunday," he said as he plopped down in front of the radio's blare. "It's church time."

It was clear to Larry that the matter was settled, at least for the time being. The old man obviously knew the territory better than anyone. Until something better came along they would just have to rely on his judgment.

Jonathan rocked back in his chair, his face a picture of satisfaction. The room resounded with the sounds of his favorite program, *The Hour of Decision* with Billy Graham. The voice of Cliff Barrows penetrated the static with familiar tones.

"So pray for Alaska during these coming days. And for those of you listening to us in that great northern state, we will look forward to seeing you in person at the Sullivan Arena in Anchorage. And now before Mr. Graham's

message, here's Bev Shea."

As the music floated into the room, it was suddenly swallowed in a burst of spits and crackles. Jonathan sat forward in the chair, straining to decipher the melody as the static increased, then ended abruptly in a loud pop. The light in the dial flickered out and a white curl of smoke drifted upward from the front louvers. The room was heavy with silence. Jonathan's mouth sagged in disbelief. He lifted himself out of the chair and shuffled to the radio. Flipping the switch several times, he studied it with furrowed brow. The radio sat silently. Jonathan reached up and gave the relic a quick slap across its top. Nothing happened. Irritated now, he hit it again with more force. The radio bounced with the sharp blow of the doubled fist. For a brief instant it sat on the shelf at an askewed angle, then suddenly the whole shelf gave way, raining down the wall an avalanche of cascading papers, books and canned goods.

Jonathan sucked his breath in with a gasp as he vainly attempted to restrain the deluge of paraphernalia. The crashing, clanking and billowing dust clouds brought a yelp from Jake as he slipped and clawed his way across the floor in desperate search of safer quarters.

"Well, crimeny-Ann!!!" the old man bellowed, his voice dying slowly with the last echo of falling items. The floor was a jumble of scattered treasures and somewhere below the dust cloud at Jonathan's feet, was the broken remnant of his radio.

Cal's eyes were wide with amazement. He looked over to his dad only to find a similar reaction. They stared at each other in disbelief. Jonathan stood at the center of the room, his arms limp at his sides. Smiles played dangerously near the corners of both the onlookers' mouths. They struggled to maintain their composure, afraid to let their emotions have free will, at least for the moment.

Chapter Seven

Early the next morning, Jonathan and Cal left Larry resting in the cabin. Jonathan thought the good weather would hold for the rest of the day, but the old man never liked to take chances. Years of mountain life had taught him that he could take advantage of a bright sun-lit morning — but not count too heavily on its carrying into the afternoon. A late summer williwaw was always possible and Jonathan didn't relish struggling up the steep mountain trail against the blast of a rain-soaked wind.

Following his well-established custom, Jonathan set a grueling pace down the face of the mountain. As the stiffness worked out of his joints, his stride lengthened.

Cal nearly ran to keep up. "Do we have to go so fast?" he gasped.

Jonathan didn't look back. "If you can't keep up, go back to the cabin," he growled. His long, wiry legs pumped along the trail.

Cal lost ground with each massive stride. By the time they reached the last of the upper meadows, he was a good sixty yards behind the man. As he watched, Jonathan turned left and crossed an old footbridge that spanned one of the clear alpine streams. Time and water had eaten away at the lumber of the walkway until it was little more than a skeletal framework of slippery planks.

With four well-placed steps, Jonathan negotiated the bridge, then turned and glared back at the lagging boy. "If you can't keep up," he bellowed, "then wait here!" The big man spun on one heel and stepped over the edge of the bluff and skittered down the steep, grassy slope.

After negotiating the bridge, Cal broke into a trot. Determined to keep up with the old man all the way to the canyon, he slipped and slid down the grassy slope, then ran up behind Jonathan. A smile tugged at Cal's lips as he noted the pleased look in the old man's eyes.

They followed the backs of several small ridges, working along the side of the mountain in a descending path that Jonathan hoped would end near the lost kayak. The old man skirted across the upper edge of the alder thickets, then with unerring skill he plunged through what looked to the boy like an impossible brush barrier. Cal grabbed hold of the back of Jonathan's heavy jacket and was pulled through the maze of tangled branches.

They broke through the thicket onto a well-established game trail that offered an open path all the way down to the river. The gnarled alders leaned over the trail with high arching limbs, but offered no resistance to the hikers at ground level. The further down the slope they traveled, the more defined the pathway became as sidetracks joined the common thoroughfare. In time, Jonathan saw it wouldn't come out exactly where he aimed to make his exit, so he led the boy off the trail.

As they entered the lower timbered section of the mountain, their angle of descent lessened. Cal could hear the sound of the rapids well below them. They crossed above the rocky narrows where the accident happened and angled toward an intersect with the river, well beyond the spot where Cal had pulled Larry from the pool. In this area the river broke free from the rocky restrictions of the narrows and flowed out onto a boulder-strewn valley, about a half-mile wide.

Cal dogged along behind the old man as they weaved their way back and forth through the spruce forest, stretching his steps out as far as possible in an attempt to match the long strides the man took. It was a futile effort, and required him to add an extra skip now and then. But he remained close on the old man's heels.

Jonathan continued to angle down canyon. "We're gonna cut off and follow this other game trail," he remarked, tossing the words over his shoulder as he pushed through the underbrush and continued his descent. Cal tagged closely behind.

When they were within a hundred yards of the water, on a slightly angled drift that would eventually bring them out to the river bank, Jonathan slowed a bit. Periodically, he would dip his head and peer under the low branches.

Cal wondered what the old man was up to. With a frown, he followed closer behind, and watched Jonathan's peculiar antics.

The old man stopped. He turned back to catch Cal's eye and he held up a weathered hand. His brow wrinkled as he watched the boy stop and silently hold his position. He nodded and turned back around and squatted, then, without glancing at the boy, he waved Cal forward.

The youngster inched his way up beside Jonathan and slipped to his knees. He looked to where the old man pointed. There was some commotion off near a small depression. At first Cal could only see a small brown shape moving around. Then, there were ears, then two sets of inquisitive eyes. Finally, a pair of long, sprightly animals appeared. They frolicked along an old streambed, turning over small rocks and digging under stones, looking for a mid-morning snack. Completely oblivious to the presence of the human observers, they loped along the rocky ditch, bumping and nuzzling each other in playful affection.

Cal was instantly enchanted. His mouth spread across his

face and his eyes danced. He leaned close to the big man, "What are they?"

Jonathan smirked. "Shhhh," he cautioned in a low whisper. "They're otters." He grinned and pointed at the larger of the pair. "That's Herman." Then he fingered the other one as she raised her head. "And that one's Geraldine."

Cal squinted at the old man. "You're fooling me."

Jonathan shook his head and poked his lips out. "I know 'em."

Cal's eyes widened. "Wow!" he exclaimed. "That's neat!"

Herman froze at the sound of the boy's ecstatic voice. The animal's tiny eyes locked onto the intruding pair. One forepaw dangled, suspended an inch or two above the ground. With ears perked, he dipped his head in several nervous jerks and chirped a warning to Geraldine.

Jonathan puckered his lips and answered the otter's nervous barks with several low, cooing whistles.

The sound of the man's calls brought an instant reaction from the pair of otters and they chirped back excitedly, bobbing their heads while they fiddle-footed from side to side on the smooth stones. Then they turned and loped away, disappearing into the lush undergrowth.

Jonathan glanced at Cal. "They weren't too sure about you," he muttered. He stood and looked down at the boy. "Otherwise, they'd have stayed around a little longer." He lifted one eyebrow. "They can smell city folks."

Cal was still amazed. His mouth hung agape and he gazed up at the old man. "You really know them?" He stood and wagged his head, then looked out to where they had disappeared. His eyes were wide. "Have you ever touched them?"

The old man snorted and adjusted his hat. "Never been closer than fifteen feet or so." He switched his rifle to his other shoulder and started out ahead of the boy again. "But I know 'em sure enough." He glanced back. "And they know me. We get along." He scanned the forest around him, sighed and clicked his tongue. "You gotta give God's creatures their due respect. They know who will, but when they ain't sure, they'd rather move on." He hesitated to make certain the boy caught his next point. "You just can't reach out and grab hold of wild things. You gotta treat 'em gentle and let 'em be." He raised his brow and nodded, then he moved on.

As they penetrated the last thicket, they stepped out onto a wide boulder-strewn basin that paralleled the river. Cal ran ahead of Jonathan and jumped to the top of one of the large rounded rocks. Almost immediately he spotted a slash of light blue cloth near the water's edge. "Hey, Jonathan! There's our stuff!" Cal leaped down from the rock and scampered across the irregular stones toward the river's edge.

The favorable weather dropped the water level steadily, leaving a swatch of scattered supplies spread along the riverbank for several hundred feet.

As Cal skidded to a halt near the blue cloth, he stared at its knotted contour. "What in the world *is* this?" he muttered. It was wrapped in soggy folds around the base of a large rock, half encased in dark-gray silt. Cal's jaw slackened. "Oh man," he moaned. "It's my sleeping bag."

Jonathan strolled toward the riverbank, weaving through the boulders. He was pleased that his trek down the mountain brought them so close to their intended goal. He paused and squatted next to a shallow pool. His brow furrowed when he spotted several pouches of sealed food partially submerged in the muddy water. His large hand sank into the murky pool. He picked up one of the foil containers and wiped it with his sleeve. He squinted and held it at arm's length. "Humph," he grunted. "Potatoes and spinach, ah-graytin." He shook his head and smirked, "Pretty fancy." His lips pursed. "City folks," he murmured.

His attention was drawn down river by Cal's shrill call.

Cal's excited shout resounded in the canyon. "Hey! Jonathan, there's the kayak!"

The old man stood and peered at the boy.

Cal was tiptoed on a high boulder, waving and pointing excitedly. The kayak was beached about fifty yards down the river from the pair. Its usual sleek outline was crumpled against a tangled nest of roots, and its shell was pierced by several splintered ribs.

The two of them spent most of the mid-day repairing the broken boat and gathering up all of the spilled supplies they were able to find. Jonathan fashioned several alder splints and inserted them next to the broken supports of the kayak. He then lashed them securely in place, providing the boat with a reasonably strong framework. Cal helped him patch the punctured skin with strips of gray tape. The old man stood back and looked at the craft. He patted Cal's shoulder. "She's sound enough. I think she'll withstand the river on down to Caribou Lake." He nudged the boy. "Come on. Let's stuff our packs with as many of the supplies as we can carry, then head back up the mountain."

Cal smiled up at the old man. "I think everything's gonna be fine now."

Jonathan didn't answer, but reached out and tousled the lad's mop of hair.

With easy steps, they followed their return path up the steep slope. Jonathan set the pace, but this time it was much more relaxed. He was sure now that the balmy weather would hold through the rest of the afternoon, and with both the boy and himself carrying loaded packs, he saw little need to press too hard. He worked his way through the thick timber of the lower slope, his attention finely honed to notice every movement of the forest around them.

Cal followed close behind, puffing under the load of his pack.

As they neared the upper stretch of timber the underbrush closed in on the trail, drastically cutting Jonathan's visibility. He moved through one cluster, then took a step and stopped short.

Cal ambled along through the trail opened by the big man. The boy had his head down and his mind wandered. He didn't notice that Jonathan had stopped and he ran into the old man's back. He jumped back. "What's wrong?" His eyes were wide.

Jonathan lifted a finger and glared at the boy. "Shhh."

Cal blinked and remembered the otters. He smiled and gazed around at the thick tangle of alders, trying to see. He flexed his shoulders trying to adjust his pack. The effort pulled the youngster off balance and he stumbled a bit and stepped off the trodden trail onto a dry branch. The twig snapped.

Jonathan's head whirled around and his jaw tightened. He held a palm up to Cal. He whispered, "Quiet now!" His lips were tight. "Stand perfectly still." He held Cal's gaze for a long moment to punctuate the importance of his command, then he carefully scanned the surrounding cover. He was unsure of just what had alerted his senses, but he had an eerie feeling that they were being watched. He cocked his head, searching out every sound. He could hear Cal's heavy breathing behind him. Nothing seemed unusual. He sucked in a breath of humid air. The atmosphere was heavy with the aroma of alder and moss, but there was something else. It was very faint, more like a memory. He tested the breathless air with short sniffs. At first there was nothing but the pungent fragrance of the vegetation — a rich mixture of leaves, sap and rotting humus. Then he caught the intruding scent again. This time stronger. The skin on the back of his neck crawled. In a smooth, quick motion, he slipped his rifle from his shoulder and brought it across his chest.

Cal frowned at the old man's tense reaction. The boy ventured a step closer and stood quietly.

There was a long moment of stilled silence, then to their right, the forest exploded with a torrent of rage. The slashing of underbrush reverberated with an angry snort and the loud clack of snapping jaws.

The pair whirled. About twenty-five yards off the trail the alders shuddered and branches snapped. In the midst of the gyrating overgrowth, a dark, awesome shadow rose up.

The towering outline of a ten-foot grizzly emerged. The raging bear glared at the intruders. He wrinkled his nostrils, flaring his wide upper lip. With a strong blast from his lungs, the bear sent a shower of saliva over the surrounding brush. His thick neck and hump hair bristled. He lunged forward. His great rolling lopes crashed through the underbrush. The gigantic bruin bore down on the startled pair.

Cal's mouth widened as he staggered back a step.

Jonathan grasped the boy's shoulder and yanked him back to his side. "Don't move!" the old man growled.

The sharp command froze Cal in his tracks.

Jonathan planted his feet in a wide stance, his shoulders square to the charging beast. He raised his gun but kept it shy of his shoulder. His jaw was stern and set, and he leaned toward the grizzly and shouted, "WHOA! Hold it right there!" His voice bellowed and resounded in the trees.

The huge beast stopped within a few yards of the frozen pair. He stood to his full height and towered over them.

Cal's wide eyes and open mouth matched his ashen complexion. He stood as stone, unmoving and gray.

The big bear poked his snout in the air and pumped it, then blasted through his nostrils.

Cal caught the rank stench of the animal's breath. The boy swallowed hard.

Jonathan's eyes narrowed and his expression remained firm. "All right, Grizz." His voice was clear and composed, "You've had your look and you've made your point. You've impressed everyone on the mountain, to be sure. But now, why don't you just back off a bit, and we'll be movin' on out of your territory." His words created smooth, melodic patterns. There was a deep air of authority in the tone. He took command and stared directly into the eyes of the beast.

The huge animal snorted again and looked down on the old man as it swayed.

Jonathan inched his rifle into a firing position. "You're on the edge of steppin' out of line here, Grizz. Go on now, or I might have to ventilate your hide." He motioned to the beast with a twist of his head.

The big bear snorted again, glanced at Cal, then dropped to all fours. His huge head swayed as he eyed the pair. Then with slow, deliberate steps, he sauntered off. He glanced over his shaggy shoulder, nervously checking on them while deep guttural growls followed an occasional sniff and snort.

Jonathan watched the retreating bear, aware of every movement. He kept his voice low and spoke out of the side of his mouth. "I don't trust him. Stay steady, boy. Don't move and don't say a thing."

Even after the animal disappeared into the foliage, the old man continued watching and listening. For a long moment everything was quiet.

Cal touched Jonathan's arm. The old man put his finger up to his lips. Cal remained silent.

After several tense minutes, Jonathan gripped Cal's upper arm and nodded. "Come on," he whispered. He looked back as they started to move away.

The pair eased their way up the path, Jonathan scanning the brush on all sides. His voice was low. "Can't trust a grizzly," he warned. "He'd just as soon come back on us from our blind side." The man's senses were piqued.

They moved silently as one unit with Cal just as close to the old man as possible. They worked their way through the heavy timber until the trail broke out onto a wide grassy hillside. Jonathan continued up the steep, open slope. Occasionally, he checked the brushy timber behind them, just to be sure.

As they reached the crest of the knoll, he stopped, removed his hat and wiped the beads of perspiration from his forehead. He studied the timber below. His shoulders heaved as he took a deep breath, relieving some of his tension. Then he glanced up and sighed. "Thank you, Lord."

Cal eyed the old man. A smile tugged at the youth's mouth. "I figured you were as mean as that bear when you stared him down and yelled at him." He gazed into Jonathan's eyes. "But you were just as scared as I was." He squinted, then frowned a bit when Jonathan didn't answer. "You could have shot him, couldn't you?"

Jonathan smirked and wiped the inside lining of his hat with his handkerchief. He replaced the rag and put the hat back on. His eyes narrowed as he peered down at the youngster. He patted his rifle. "I don't think that really would have made much difference, son." His gaze turned back for a final glance at the timber. "A man's got a right to fear a grizzly. They don't usually let up as easy as that one did." He nodded and looked up. "Somebody was watchin' out for us." He looked back down into the boy's face. "Let's get goin'." He turned up the slope again. After just two steps, the old man paused and looked back. He stared at Cal, then he tilted his head with a smile. "You know, son. You did real good back there." His eyes sparkled at the lad. "If you'd have run, or screamed, it may not have turned out so good." He nodded at the boy once again and smiled broadly. "Yup, you did real good." He winked and began the trek again.

Cal fell in close behind the old man, then eased up to walk next to him. Jonathan glanced down at the boy at his side and a slight smile appeared on his cracked lips. He nodded and they continued up the grassy slope. Cal felt close to Jonathan and wanted to know more about the man. He looked up at his frizzled beard and wondered about him. "The boy in the picture book, did he use to live here?"

Jonathan was visibly shaken by the question. He kept his steady pace, his eyes watching the ground in front of them. "Years ago." His words were clipped.

Cal pressed him. "The lady, did she die?"

Jonathan frowned and took several strides before he answered. "Been a long time now."

"Did your boy die too?"

"Nope." He pushed under an overhanging branch and held it for Cal.

The youngster slipped under the man's arm and waited until he let go of the branch and turned to walk next to him again. "Does he come up here and see you much?"

The old man sighed and looked down at Cal. "I haven't seen my son in years." His lips pinched together and he blinked several times. "We took our separate ways after his mother died." He stared across the mountain ridge in an unfocused gaze. "I guess he blames me for not living down in the city where she could get proper care. He just didn't understand." Jonathan's voice seemed hollow. He cleared his throat and straightened. "Anyway, he's got his own world. He never found much use for the wilderness when he got older." His mouth felt dry. "We never could see eye-to-eye," he grunted. "He was always hard-headed and difficult. He just won't . . " He didn't finish. He figured he'd said enough.

The trail narrowed as they reached a large stand of alder brush. Cal fell in behind Jonathan again and they walked single-file through the thick cover.

Jonathan looked over his shoulder. "What about you, boy?" He grinned. "What's your story?"

Cal smirked. "I guess me and my dad don't see things the same way either." He stepped over a fallen log and hurried to catch up to the big man again. "My mom and dad are getting a divorce. He brought me on this trip to tell me about it." Cal stared at the back of Jonathan's shaggy head. "I guess this trip was supposed to make me feel better about it." He shuffled along the path, then kicked at a stone. "But, I don't care anymore." The boy continued following in the shadow of the old man. He blinked the mist from his eyes. "Dad promised that we'd take a trip like this every year." He moved up close behind Jonathan. "Maybe we could come back and visit you again."

Jonathan grunted and moved on, the boy staying close on his heels.

Chapter Eight

It was early, but downtown Anchorage was busy. Tall buildings with ultra-modern glass fronts towered over the milling crowds, mirroring the late summer patchworks of green and brown that spread across the Chugach Mountains. The thriving city stood a world apart from Mystery Mountain. Many who scurried along its canyons of cement and glass would never set foot beyond the surrounding peaks, content enough just to know they were there and that somewhere beyond their summits lay the domain of the moose and the bear. Theirs was a world of business and competition and international markets anxious for the treasures to be found in the Great Land.

Carolyn felt tighter than usual as she swung the Blazer into the clinic parking lot. As soon as she parked it, she shuddered. An early morning chill crawled down her back and another wave of nausea swept through the pit of her stomach. Beads of perspiration broke out across her upper lip and under her auburn hair at the base of her neck.

Gradually, the sickness passed and she took several deep breaths to renew her energy. She glanced at her watch — nine-thirty, half an hour to kill before her appointment with

Dr. Blake. She frowned and gazed out at the tall buildings. "This is silly," she muttered. "I hate being early. Why am I here so early?" The question didn't have an answer, or at least she couldn't readily bring it to the fore. Her slender fingers tilted the mirror so she could look at her face. The wave of nausea had made its mark on her tired brow. A sheen of perspiration around her mouth and across her forehead glistened in the morning sunlight.

Carolyn poked out her lower lip and blew a curly wisp of hair out of her vision. She reached under the locks overlapping her collar and fluffed them up, away from her damp neck. She smirked and glanced down into her purse, then looked at herself again. After dusting her forehead with a few quick swipes of her makeup pad, she tilted her head to check her blush. Her full lips twisted and she threw her compact back into her purse. The face she saw mirrored there would have to do. She was tired of trying.

She sighed as she eyed her reflection one last time. "You're not a pretty sight," she muttered. Shrugging, she straightened the mirror and got out of the Blazer.

She crossed the street and subconsciously ambled down the block to kill some time. Out of the corner of her eye she noticed her reflection in one of the glazed windows and stopped to gawk at the image. To her, the reflection was that of a stranger, the caricature of a lonely, frustrated woman who had nothing left to inspire a future. She felt mystically distant.

Carolyn glanced at her watch and noted twenty-five more minutes to burn. She peered again at her swollen image in the window which reflected a blur of passing traffic and the rush of people hurrying to meet their appointed times. Her nose wrinkled as she stared at her frontal view, then turned to profile herself, pressing the smock over the slightly rounded tummy. She straightened and glanced around, suddenly aware of people looking her way. She ambled on down the street.

Without conscious thought, Carolyn noticed how close she

was to the building which housed Larry's third-floor office. She hesitated, then smiled as she remembered that they had chosen the clinic because of its close proximity to his work. It had seemed very convenient. But now, nothing looked convenient. In fact, Carolyn thought the office building looked grey and overbearing, with an air about it that made her feel uneasy. She squinted as she stood outside the building, allowing her eyes to move down until she was gazing at the brass-trimmed entrance. Suddenly, as though pushed from behind, an impulse took her through the door and over to the elevator. She pressed the button and waited. The spacious lobby was tastefully decorated. Above the large center table, a brass-trimmed chandelier hung from a high sculptured ceiling. Even the overstuffed chairs circling the perimeter of the lobby had brass trim. They sat bleakly empty. "Someone must have had a thing for brass," she muttered. Just then the elevator doors opened. Two young executive types stepped past Carolyn as she entered.

When the doors slid open on the third floor and Carolyn stepped out, she remembered she'd only been there once before, yet she felt she knew which way to turn and what was ahead. As she made her way down the hallway to an open area, the place wasn't as she had remembered it. Now it seemed larger, ominous, like an old deserted castle. The hollow open area echoed her approach.

A receptionist seated at the entrance to the open area stopped typing and smiled up at Carolyn's frown. "May I help you?"

Carolyn stood mute and glanced around. Her eyes darted to a large picture, then she blinked and looked at the puzzled typist. "Uh, yes." She tried to smile, but it seemed she was in a daze. "I - I'm here to see Laurie Matthews."

The receptionist nooded politely and smiled, leaning forward and pointing to her left. "She's in the first cubicle on your right."

Carolyn looked that way and frowned. She hesitated and swallowed hard.

The receptionist stretched her neck and lifted her chin in a patronizing way. "Did you need me to take you in, dear?"

Carolyn heisted her nose a bit. "No! No, thank you. I can manage."

The receptionist returned to her typing.

Carolyn took two hesitant steps. She was drawn by an irresistible mixture of anger and intrigue, but a part of her was mometarily cautious. Then, just as suddenly as she had entered the building, she passed briskly through a doorway and turned toward the first module on her right, stepping quickly into the temporary office space.

The woman seated behind the desk was very young and quite pretty. Thick blond hair brushed the tops of her shoulders. Her makeup was flawless and her lips were full and sensuous. She didn't seem the type Larry would have wanted.

Carolyn stood silently in front of the desk.

The young woman stapled a sheaf of papers and looked up. She smiled warmly. "Hi. May I help you?"

Carolyn's anger rose. She stared at the youthful woman but said nothing.

Laurie twisted in her seat. "Ah," she hesitated and smiled, "I bet you're looking for personnel." She stood. "They're on this floor all right, but they're at the opposite end of the hall." She pointed with a very slender, very feminine finger. "You should have turned left when you got off the elevator." She nodded and sat down. "It happens all the time." She acted as though the conversation was finished as she picked up her pen and checked over some papers.

When Carolyn didn't leave, the young woman slowly looked up into her glaring eyes. "Do we know each other?" She licked her lips. "Is there something . . ."

"Laurie Matthews?" Carolyn's eyes blazed. She hated to utter the name.

Laurie swallowed and set her pen down. "Yes," she admitted. "I - I'm Ms. Matthews."

Carolyn forced a shallow smile. "Well, Mizzz Mathews,

I was thinking of applying for your job."

Although Laurie's frown deepened, she was still very pretty.

Carolyn thought the woman's shoulders were too large for her frame. Maybe she was just looking for imperfection. She twisted her neck, tossing her hair slightly. "I'm a good typist. And I'm sure I could look busy checking unimportant papers all day." She leaned across the desk and looked directly into the woman's bewildered expression. "How would you be at my job? Are you good enough to take care of babies? Could you take care of my husband, *full-time?*"

Laurie's mouth dropped open and her eyes darted back and forth, searching Carolyn's face for an explanation for the insinuations. "I don't understand . . ."

Carolyn glared down at her. "Well, I'm with you on that one." Suddenly her hatred broke and she felt tears well up deep inside. She whirled quickly and ran out of the office.

Laurie sat stunned momentarily, then with weak knees she rose.

At the elevator, Carolyn slapped at the buttons. She was desperate. She knew she'd made a fool of herself and her eyes brimmed with salty tears. Her mind raced. She'd acted like a child and now she wanted to run, to get away, far away. She wanted to be out of the building, lost in the city, away from the woman who had invaded her privacy. To Carolyn, Laurie Matthews had stolen the most intimate moments of her life. She could have Larry. It all was history now. Then, the incident, what she and Larry once had — it was lost forever. Nothing could recapture the past. She only wanted to be away from anything that reminded her of Larry and the ache that had replaced her deep love. It was forever gone. Nothing, nor anyone, could erase the scars gouged into her spirit. She knew she'd remember and hate until the day she died.

As the elevator door slid open, she hurried inside. She could hear footsteps clicking, echoing in the castle-like halls. It was dark and dank, and desperation and despair were ready to attack. The heels were clicking closer now. Carolyn frantically slapped at the buttons but the doors stubbornly refused to close. She struck the control panel once again. Tears streaked down her soft cheeks. She quickly wiped at them. The clicking echoed louder and she melted against the darkest corner of the elevator. Her lips were tight. "Oh, God, close these doors," she muttered. "Hurry."

The clicking stopped and Laurie appeared in front of the elevator. She looked at Carolyn tucked in the corner.

Carolyn straightened, trying to hold her head erect. She made an absurd effort to appear calm and composed, but her heart beat wildly and she felt her cheeks flush. She tried to glare at Laurie, but the hurt was too close to the surface and she felt her lower lip quivering. She bit it. When she looked into Laurie's eyes, Carolyn saw the evidence of hurt, sorrow and regret. The young woman no longer appeared as the sensuous floozy Carolyn had seen in her imagination.

Laurie was vulnerable and aching. She too was on the verge of tears. "M - Mrs. Sanders?" She swallowed. "Are you Carolyn Sanders?"

Carolyn couldn't answer and the two women stared at each other through the blur of tears as the elevator doors slid closed.

Within a few minutes Carolyn reluctantly arrived at her appointment. She had wiped her face in the reflection of the polished brass trim of the office building, hurried down to the clinic and was ushered in immediately.

Now, she scanned the empty ceiling of the small examination room. The table felt cold and abrupt under her back, and the tissue paper covering the plastic pad rustled with her every move. She tried to lie still. Dr. Blake's pen scratched as she filled out the medical chart.

Carolyn wanted to get her mind off Laurie, so she made conversation. "I hear that a fast heartbeat means it's a girl?"

Dr. Blake turned around and smiled. Her round face made Carolyn feel comfortable. She looked back at the chart and then up to Carolyn again. "That's what people like to think." She made a mark on the chart, then allowed it to sag to her side. Her smile broadened. "Has Cal put his order in for a little sister?"

Carolyn couldn't untangle her mind. Although she tried to make coherent conversation, her mind was muddled. "Sometimes I think I can feel it move." She wagged her head. "I know that can't be. It's much too early."

Dr. Blake frowned at her. She placed her pen under the metal snap of her clipboard.

Carolyn continued to stare at the ceiling for a long silent moment. "I heard about this woman who had an abortion, and she was into her fifth month." She shifted her position on the table and stared at the doctor. "Is that possible?"

Dr. Blake leaned against the counter and studied Carolyn. She tried to scan beneath the surface to find the root of the question. Pushing away from the counter and putting the clipboard on it, she turned and looked directly into Carolyn's eyes, taking a deep breath. "Well, Alaskan Law allows for termination of pregnancy up to twenty-one weeks." She held up a finger. "If circumstances warrant it."

Carolyn leaned up on one elbow. "Who determines whether the circumstances warrant it?"

Doctor Blake shook her head. "Believe it or not, the mother does, mostly."

Carolyn sighed and allowed her body to roll back so she was looking up at the light fixture. "When is it safest?" She pushed her head up and looked at the other woman. "I mean, am I past time?"

After leaving the clinic, Carolyn drove straight home and turned the Blazer up the quiet street. She was exhausted. Her eyes felt heavy and she longed for the solitude of an empty house and a hot soothing bath. When she glanced up the street, her dream of retreating into silence was shattered. Her mother's car was parked at the head of the driveway and she knew that the inevitable questions and counter questions would have to be answered before she got any peace and quiet. She slumped behind the wheel feeling terribly ill-equipped to cope with a needless rehash of an insolvable situation.

By the time Carolyn parked and entered the house, she had resigned herself to the inevitable. Her mother was seated at the kitchen table. She forced a polite smile. "Hello, Mother."

"Maybe today you should just call me Marian, or Mrs. Thomas."

Carolyn's eyes rolled and her hands fell limply at her sides. "Oh, come on, Mother. Just because I want to handle my own problems in my own way, by myself, is no reason to feel I've left you out of my life."

Mrs. Thomas was a woman whose style was direct and to the point. Early years of Alaskan homesteading had long since stripped away any tendency toward delicacy. When she felt a subject needed to be handled, she didn't fool around, but went directly to the point. "Then maybe you'd like to tell your father about this divorce. I don't think I can break anymore bad news this week."

"Mother!" Carolyn whined. "You have to tell him. I can't face what he'll say." She scowled at the older woman. "I have enough trouble having to listen to your chiding."

Marian looked at her daughter's eyes. "You've been crying, I see. Come and sit. We need to talk."

Carolyn reluctantly sat at the table. "Mother, I'm tired. I want to take a bath and lie down for a while. I've had a — a trying morning."

Marian barely heard her. "You know, Hon, this one is going to take more than guts and anger to get out of the pits." Her eyes softened as she leaned on her elbows and looked into Carolyn's face. "Why don't you ask for help on this one?"

Carolyn felt a strange surge of frustration. She pushed her chair back from the table and stood. "I've got to go into the living room and lie down a bit." She shook her head and looked back over her shoulder as she passed through the doorway. "We're past counseling, Mom!" She took a deep breath and held it for an instant. Her voice rose as she called back to the kitchen. "It all becomes empty words, nothing more!" She flopped down on the couch and cradled one of its tasseled pillows under her chin.

Marian followed her into the living room. She eyed Carolyn. "I wasn't talking about my counseling you. I was talking about God."

Carolyn's face was etched with resentment. "What can He do!" She rolled on her side. "We've got a lot of broken promises. I've been devastated and that can't be erased." She shrugged. "Hey, it happens. It's the kind of world we live in."

Marian's lips moved in the silence that hovered over the room. She watched Carolyn, then said, "You left God on a side road a long way back." She hesitated. "He can mend this . . ."

Carolyn jerked her eyes to attach themselves to the older woman's. "Can God erase the last thirty days as though they never happened?" Her lips tightened. "Can He blot out Laurie Matthews?" she snapped. She buried her face in the pillow.

Marian's voice was low and soothing. "No, I don't think He'll do that, but He can give you hope for a future." She stepped around the coffee table and sat down beside Carolyn. She stroked the tresses of her hair and whispered, "Listen, Kiddo. If you don't give up all this hurt that is inside of you, it's going to turn to scar tissue and you're going to get harder and harder. You'll be like granite by the time you're my age. You won't trust anybody." She stopped stroking Carolyn's hair and patted her shoulder.

Carolyn moved the pillow so that her cheek rested on it and she stared across the room. The silence grew as neither one chose to speak. Her mother's hand moved over her shoulders and down her back. The tenderness of her touch was the first Carolyn had felt in a long time. She responded to the back rub. "Can you massage a little lower, Mom? I've been having some real trouble in my lower back."

Marian kept rubbing. "Why don't you give it to the Lord, Honey?"

Carolyn stared at the far wall. Her voice was deeply emotional. "If it was only that easy," she muttered.

"Honey, it's not easy. But it's real." She stopped rubbing and smiled at her daughter's profile. "I guarantee it's a whole lot better." She tapped Carolyn's shoulder. "Hey, pride is a mighty poor substitute for what God can do."

Carolyn sighed and closed her eyes.

Marian stood. "Well, I'd better be going." She slipped her coat on. "I can see I'm in for some heavy praying." She headed for the door and stopped. For a moment she was reflective, then she turned and looked at her daughter. "If you've still got the good sense that you were raised with, you'll get on your knees too."

She opened the door, but paused once again. "Does Cal know?"

Carolyn nodded reluctantly. "He knows. I saw it in his eyes when he and Larry got on the plane."

Marian smiled slightly. "Think about his future," she said.

Chapter Nine

Up in the antiquated mining town, old Jake barked and Cal ran after him. The boy's wild laughter echoed off Mystery Mountain and bounced around the ridges.

Inside the cabin, Jonathan stopped hammering to listen to the youthful sounds. He grinned at Larry. "Yup," he said, "that boy of yours is a good one."

Larry looked up from his work at the table. He smiled and shook his head, then he turned his chair a bit so he could talk more directly to the old man. He watched the big hammer drive another nail into the shelving. Larry's eyebrows raised. "Don't you think you've put enough nails in that thing?"

Jonathan jerked on the sturdy shelving. He gave Larry an almost childish grin. "I don't expect we'll see it come down again." He jerked on it once more, then pointed the hammer's handle at the broken radio. "If you can fix that squawk-box, I'll listen to my heart's content, and I won't have to worry about it fallin' anymore." Putting the hammer on the shelf, he took out his handkerchief to wipe his heavy brow. The old man appraised Larry as he watched him tinker with the shattered radio. He thought the man had recovered nicely.

Larry raised his eyebrows and peered into the tangle of colored wires. Several components were bent, or shaken from their sockets. He lowered his head and pushed his fingers into a tiny opening among the wires to withdraw a small tube. It was intact and looked all right. "I'll do fine with her if she hasn't got any messed up tubes." He held the small glass bulb up to the light. His mouth twitched and he snorted. "It looks okay, but you never know. This one was loose and lying on the chassis." He turned the back of the old receiver toward Jonathan. "See where it's bent, there next to the socket?" As he watched Jonathan squint, he realized the old man had trouble seeing at close range. He turned the radio back to continue his efforts. "Anyway, that bend must have popped this tube out. If the socket's not too damaged, or the chassis isn't warped, then we may be in business."

In the distance, Cal's laughter resounded and Jonathan glanced up at the door. He didn't look at Larry, but talked to him. "That sure is a fine boy." He turned his attention back to the radio repair. "You know, in a way I owe my life to that boy."

Larry squinted into the dark chassis and kept working with the tube. He muttered, "He's a good boy all right." He picked up the longnose pliers.

Jonathan rubbed his whiskers. "Like I said, he carried his share of supplies and kept up with me real good." He snickered. "Even with all I put on him, I didn't hear one peep of complaining." Jonathan shifted to try to see into the chassis. "Not many youngsters like that around anymore." He poked his head down next to Larry's so he could get a better view of the maze of wires and tubes. "I'll tell you, I've encountered a few grizzlies in my time, but I've never been in a tighter spot than this last one." He leaned back and gave Larry some elbow room. "Scared as that boy was, he did what I told him and never blinked an eye."

Larry stopped working with the pliers and laid them on

the table. His eyes searched the tools spread around and he blinked. He shook his head a bit.

"You okay?"

Larry nodded. "Uh-huh. I'm looking for that commonhead."

Jonathan pointed at it. "Near your right elbow."

Larry grasped it. "Thanks."

Jonathan pushed his chair back. "How about some coffee?" he suggested.

"Sure," Larry muttered. He glanced up at the bigger man. "If you're going to have a cup, then I'll join you."

Jonathan smiled and got up. As he prepared the brew, he talked easily. "I sure am glad you're trying to fix that old radio. It's kinda special you know."

Larry leaned back and glanced over his shoulder. "Well, I think I've just about got it." He looked at Jonathan's delighted smile. "These are temporary connections, but they should hold for a while." He rubbed his chin and thought for a moment. "I can patch these cracks in the cabinet with this electrical tape, but it'll come loose in no time in the dampness." He snapped his fingers and turned around in his chair.

Jonathan glanced at the excited look in Larry's eyes, but continued pouring the coffee. "What's on your mind?" He brought the cups to the table.

"I've got a great idea. Somewhere at home, I've got a battery-powered, all-band shortwave radio. That would solve your problems." He grinned and lifted his cup. "When Cal and I get home, I'll pack that baby up and see that you get it."

Jonathan smiled, and yet he felt a twinge of guilt.

Larry caught the look in the old man's eyes. "It's a used rig but it works fine and I haven't used it in quite awhile. It would be just the thing for up here."

Jonathan nodded and then looked over at the old instrument. "That's mighty kind," he muttered. "I'd really appreciate a radio like that — one that works all the time." He sighed and stroked the cracked cabinet. "But my boy, he made this one when he was just fifteen. It will be kinda sad to retire it." The old man's eyes misted a bit and he blinked. The moment was silent and the pair stared at the cracked wooden case.

Finally Jonathan cleared his throat, sniffed and pushed his chair back. He grabbed the radio and put it back up on the shelf. His mood lightened. "That's a lot better." He gathered up some of the other stuff that had lined the shelf. "It's always amazed me, how a radio picks up voices and music out of the air and we can't hear anything until we turn it on." He looked into Larry's eyes. "Ethan, that's my boy, knew how it worked. He sat me down and drew diagrams and tried to explain it to me, but I couldn't catch on." He turned back to his trinkets and lined them neatly. "Guess that was the day I knew my boy was smarter than me." He dusted off the photo album with his sleeve and put it on the upper shelf. He looked at the radio again. "Looks like she's sung her last song now."

"Maybe not," Larry assured. "Why don't we wait until evening, when there's less interference and see how well we can pick up something?" He smiled. "Anyway, I think she'll work for a few more programs — at least, I hope, until I can get the shortwave set to you."

Jonathan sighed and turned back to seat himself at the table. He fingered his cup as he talked. "You sure you want to do that?"

Larry's mouth broke into a wide smile. "You'd be doing me a favor to take it off my hands. I've got to get rid of some things at the house soon anyway."

Jonathan sipped his coffee and eyed the younger man. He lowered his cup and looked down into the dark liquid. "The boy told me you folks were thinking of doing some rearranging at your place." He smirked. "Splittin' up ain't the answer."

Larry flushed at the old man's direct opinion. He was surprised by Jonathan's willingness to pry into his family affairs. "W-well," Larry stammered, "we - we've been going through some difficult times lately. It's been very unsettling." He cleared his throat. "Anyway, Cal has things a little confused," he lied.

The old man sipped his coffee and looked over his cup at Larry. The silence was broken by Cal's distant laughter and Jake's barking. Jonathan looked up toward the shelf, then back to Larry. "You know, that old radio taught me plenty over the years. You take the *Hour of Decision* program." His eyes twinkled. "You know, old Billy Graham." He snickered. "Well, that old boy can come up with a lot of stuff to let a man chew on." He wagged his head. "He even says God is kinda like those radio waves." He hesitated. "Always out there, but you've got to tune them in."

Larry watched the man stop and sip his coffee. He could see into the depths of Jonathan's determined look. Larry's throat constricted and he felt uneasy.

Jonathan didn't notice, as he lowered his cup. "Seems to me a now-an'-then father just won't do the trick with a lad like that. Take my word for it. If you're not around, after a while, they're not around much either." He paused in deep thought. "Things and miles, they sure can get in the way." He blinked. "Problems happen. Then we make our decision about their solution. Oh, at the time it seems right, but suddenly a man finds he's lost everything." He shook his head and his eyes lowered. "Nobody's left, not even his son." He blinked again. "The time comes when you want to have your kid around, and you find out that he's not even your friend anymore." He looked down into the coffee left in the bottom of his cup. The room was silent.

Cal's shout to the dog jarred the old man. He sat up straight again. "Guess I better go check on those two." He wiped one corner of his eye, rose quickly and left the cabin.

Larry watched his back move out the door. Then it was shut and he sat in the stillness of the empty room.

Cal lay on the soft bed of tundra and studied a soaring eagle, gliding effortlessly on the breeze, turning in long, graceful loops against the dark blue sky. With only a slight tilting of his flared tail feathers, the regal bird climbed steadily, circling higher, until it topped the highest pinnacles. In unerring flight, its wings swept it over the jagged fingers of the summit as they caught the full blast of the upper winds. Cal squinted as he watched the majestic bird soar out of sight.

After a moment, he sighed, rolled over and pushed himself to his feet. Jake jumped up, ready to play some more. Cal looked out over the landscape of jagged rocks. It was an awesome sight to behold. He looked down at the German shepherd. "Come on, Jake. Let's take a look around."

As soon as Cal started toward the distant, weathered buildings, Jake took out ahead of him. Soon, they were weaving through the old structures and scattered piles of rusty machinery. Cal was fascinated. He spotted a few interesting pieces of metal and stopped to inspect them while Jake trotted on ahead.

After fingering the rust-flaked metal, he threw the pieces back down and his eyes gazed further down the slope. He caught a reflection near a large angular rock. "Gold," he muttered, and ran to the spot and knelt. A shiny metallic rim arched gracefully above the surface of the soil. Cal reached out and carefully touched the protruding circle of brass. Its edge was smooth and shaped like the side of a small bowl. With care, he began to scrape the soil to one side. Within a few minutes, he was turning the fascinating object back and forth in the afternoon light. Its surface was tarnished, nearly black except for the upper edge which had been polished to a bright golden hue by exposure to the wind. The bowl was attached to the top of a small rounded canister. The object was badly dented and flattened on one side. Cal held it close to his face and screwed up his mouth. "It sure isn't gold." His young brow furrowed, then he figured he knew what it was. Even though badly misshapen, it appeared to be a small antique lamp. He stuffed it into his coat pocket, thinking Jonathan would know what it was used for and maybe who had owned it.

Cal was suddenly brought to the present by Jake's barking. The dog had turned back to see where the boy was. He barked incessantly until Cal waved at him, then turned and trotted off.

"Hey, Jake," Cal shouted. "Where ya goin'?" The dog didn't stop, but barked his answer. "Hey, Jake!" Cal stretched his neck and watched the shepherd.

Jake appeared to be on a mission of his own. He wasn't interested in finding gold, or digging up old, useless lamps. He had something else in mind.

When the dog made a sharp turn and disappeared between two sheds, Cal took off after him. He sped down the descending slip and darted around the same corner Jake had used to make his exit. Cal stopped, puffing and gasping. Seeing Jake's tail disappear into one of the old buildings, Cal took out after him again. He ran up to the building and stopped short of the rugged old door. The boy was suddenly very cautious. He peered in and searched the part he could see. Nothing seemed too scary, so he ventured in. Between the dog's teeth was a bone he had hidden in the old building between some loose boards that provided a convenient exit to the outside. In a moment he and his prize were gone.

"Jake. Come here, boy." Cal put his hands on his hips and muttered. "He thinks I'm gonna steal his bone." He shrugged, then caught sight of the far wall. He was instantly transfixed. His mouth opened. "Wow!" he gasped. The rough wooden cross and the bench with the large Bible was beyond his comprehension. The room was unlike any of the tumbled-down buildings strewn across the ridge. It was clear to the boy that this was a very special place. Cal swallowed and slowly scanned the surrounding area. The piles of rusted equipment scattered around the shed looked out of place. His eyes were drawn back to the cross and the Bible. He felt odd. He wasn't frightened, but somehow he sensed that there was an unusual, unseen quality about the place. His head swiveled around to see if anyone was behind him, then

he turned back to the Bible. Without realizing it, he had stepped over into the serene atmosphere to inspect the book. He leaned over and lifted the frayed front cover. Inside were yellowed pages that had been soiled with use. He cocked his head to read the faded inscription. "Presented with love, to Edna Jane Lewis, by Jonathan K. Lewis." He squinted. "June 14, 1939," he smiled. "Edna Jane," he whispered. "That's her name." Cal heard heavy footsteps. He quickly shut the cover and whirled to face the doorway.

Jonathan entered and looked at the boy with a canted head.

"I was just looking around," Cal said sheepishly. "Jake came in here to get a bone, and I . . ."

The old man shrugged. "Don't worry about it." He went to the workbench and fiddled around for a minute, then glanced at the boy.

Cal eyed the cross and Bible again then looked back at the old man. The boy was smiling slightly, but it was mixed with genuine confusion. "Is this a church?"

Jonathan turned back to the bench and dumped the contents of one of the boxes out, sorting through the fittings. "Come here when I have a need," he mumbled.

Cal stepped a few paces toward the center of the room and looked back at the display. "How can you have a church without people?"

Jonathan kept his back toward the boy. The honesty of the question caused his sorting fingers to pause briefly. He pondered the thought for a moment before he began placing the fittings back into the box.

"Is this where you pray?" Cal asked, pressing his inquiry further.

"Yep."

Cal paced slowly across the floor to the far side of the room and looked up through the gaping hole in the metal roof. He watched as a gray cloud drifted across the deep blue sky. He turned back toward the old man. "I don't think my dad prays," he admitted.

By then, Jonathan had located the needed coupler. He turned toward the boy and leaned against the bench. He studied the lad with interest. Turning the small pipe coupler over in his palm several times, he smiled and stepped toward the center of the room. He placed his hand on Cal's shoulder and stooped down. The old man looked directly into the youngster's eyes. "Well," he said with a wink, "maybe he ain't never stared down a bear before."

Cal's eyes sparkled and his face broke into a broad grin. "Yeah!" he shouted, "That's it." He slapped his side and burst into laughter. Then just as quickly, his attention was caught when his hand hit the object in his pocket. He pulled the prize from his coat pocket.

Jonathan was genuinely surprised. "Hey, what you got there?" His mouth opened. "Why, I haven't seen one of them old miner's lamps in years. Where'd you get it?"

Cal handed it to him. He was beaming. "I dug it out of the dirt on the side of the hill." He swung around to point in the direction.

Jonathan held Cal's prize up to the light streaming through the roof. "Yessiree! This is the genuine article all right."

"What did the miners use it for?" Cal asked. He reached up and touched it inquisitively.

"Oh, hey, when this mine first opened, we used carbide lamps to see in them dark shafts." He looked up. "That was years ago." A twinkle set in Jonathan's eyes. "Long time before you were born." He eyed it again. "Nobody's used anything like this for a long time now." He held the lamp up against Cal's forehead. "Let's see how you'd look with a carbide lamp lighting your path." He held it there and leaned back to scrutinize the boy. His other hand scratched at his beard as he looked him over. "Eh," he grunted, "don't know if I'll hire you or not." He reached out and grabbed Cal's upper arm. "Kinda scrawny for a miner."

Cal flexed his muscle. "How's that?"

Jonathan laughed and handed the lamp back to Cal. "If I were you, I'd take good care of it. You'll never see another one like it."

Chapter Ten

By sunset, dark clouds had moved in from the west, casting deep shadows across the lower hill country and shrouding the uppermost spires of Mystery Mountain with their angry cloak.

Jonathan spent the last part of the afternoon preparing for the storm he was certain would blanket the high country. Because the weather had been unseasonably good for the last few weeks, he was convinced that a severe storm was on its way which would change the weather pattern and christen the upper slopes with the first touch of autumn.

The wind howled around the corner as Jonathan burst into the cabin with more wood. "Ooooeeee!" He pushed the door shut with his rear end. Jake lifted his head and Cal grinned up at the old man, eager for his return. The big man smiled at the youngster and then glanced at Larry who looked tired and a bit drawn. There was a heaviness in the air and Jonathan tried to lighten the mood. "Good weather is just nature's way of saving up." He dropped the wood next to the stove. "When the time is right, and she saves up enough, she'll sneak around the corner and clobber you with something like this." He rubbed his beard and bent to grab one of the split logs and throw it into the stove. He glanced over at Cal. "Well, it won't take long to rustle up something to eat." He smiled. "Leftovers."

As the wind whistled through the rickety old buildings and across the ridge, a light rain started.

Within an hour, a steady sheet of large drops pelted the windows of the cabin and created drumrolls on the corrugated roof. Everything popped, rattled, and groaned under the heavy rain-filled gusts that shouted their way through the mining camp, swirling and moaning up the side of the steep rock buttress.

Jonathan had supplied the cabin with a liberal stack of dry wood, so it was warm and comfortable within the walls of the tiny shelter. The lantern filled the cabin with a soft orange glow. As the three of them sat around the table, they talked openly. Jonathan had discovered conversation again. The old man was unmistakably delighted to have the pair staying with him, and when there was a lull in the conversation, he glanced at Cal. "Hey, where's that lamp you found?"

Cal chewed and swallowed his last bite of dinner. "It's still in my coat pocket," he gulped.

Jonathan turned to Larry. "Wait till you see this." He looked at Cal. "Run and fetch it." He pushed his plate to the side while Cal scrambled to retrieve the relic.

As he did, Jonathan talked to Larry. "You feelin' all right?"

Larry smiled weakly and sipped some coffee. "I guess I'm as good as can be expected for now." He put the cup down. "Maybe a little tired, but I'll be okay."

Cal came back to the table and handed the lamp to the old man. He'd been sitting on a wooden crate, and he pulled it up closer to Jonathan's elbow.

The grizzled old man held the lamp up near the lantern so he could inspect it closely. As he turned it he mumbled, "Look at that." He smiled and glanced at the pair, then back to the metal gem. He lowered it and handed it to Larry. "Bet you never seen one of them before." As Larry looked it over, Jonathan leaned closer to Cal and whispered secretively,

"Where'd you say you found it?"

Cal's voice was low, following the secretiveness. "Up on the side of the hill." He glanced at his dad, then continued. "It was buried just below the big rocky point."

Larry handed it back to the old man. "Do you recognize it?" he asked.

Jonathan wrinkled his nose. "Naw. It looks just like all the others." He put it on the table. "It must have come from the north shaft. It's up near the top of that rock wall." His chin jutted out and his beard shook. He leaned back and tilted his chair and rocked a little. His stare went through the lantern's flame, deep into the past. His mind scanned images long lost in the maze of past years. Without changing his distant stare, Jonathan recounted scenes rusted in time. "We bored and gouged that tunnel clean through to the heart of Mystery Mountain."

Cal's eyes were alight. "Did you find any gold up there?"

Jonathan sat up. His distant gaze was broken by the question. He pursed his lips. "Nothin' worth the effort. At least on that side of the mountain. We were sure we'd find the mother lode in there somewhere." He shook his silvery head. "But we never did." He sighed. "I ran one crew and old man Sweeny, he ran the other. Between the two of us, we cut tunnels all over that side of the mountain. We criss-crossed back and forth off the mainshaft until it was like a rat's nest in there." He smirked. "Finally, the company pulled off that side of the mountain. Said it was a lost cause." Jonathan leaned back in his chair and chuckled to himself. "Sweeny," he continued, "he sure didn't like that much. That old digger, he kept insistin' the big strike was in there somewhere. We all but had to drag him out of that black hole." He grinned.

Cal's eyes were wide. "But, did you ever find the gold?"

Larry leaned forward and pushed his plate out of the way. His interest piqued. "You did, didn't you?" he echoed.

"Yes, indeed," Jonathan said. He was dragging out the suspense as long as his audience would allow it. Cupping his hands behind his head, he rocked his chair a little. His eyes sparkled with the memory and the interest of the pair. "Well, I'll tell you. We took millions in gold out of these hills. The company prospered, and a few of the miners did well for themselves too. But old man Sweeny, he was sure we never hit the real glory hole. Kept insistin' it was back on the other side, somewhere in the north shaft." Jonathan wagged his head and sat up toward the table again. "He used to go back up there on his own time and scratch around back in that black maze. Only light he had was one just like this one." He tapped the lamp. "One thing about old man Sweeny I'll always remember. He had a habit of singin' down in the bowels of a mine." Jonathan snickered. "Couldn't carry a tune worth spitting at, but he sure could make the mountain moan." He chuckled at his own recall. "Sometimes, we'd hear that old man up there at night. He'd be bellowin' somewhere deep in that pit. Sounded like some weird wind howlin'." Suddenly, he leaned forward and picked up the lamp. His face grew solemn and he blinked a few times. He licked at his moustache and glanced at Larry. "You know, there's still a mystery up there that's never been solved."

"Is that why they call it Mystery Mountain?" Cal asked.

Jonathan turned to look into Cal's excited eyes. He simply nodded very slowly. His voice lowered toward a whisper. "One day, old man Sweeny turned up missin'. We looked everywhere. All his stuff was still in the dormitory, so we figur'd he must be about." His shaggy eyebrows raised slightly. "Someone thought they had heard him up in the north shaft the night before. We searched all through those tunnels." The old man hesitated and looked from Cal to Larry and back again. "Only thing we ever found," he muttered, "was his carbide headlamp." He took the lamp in his hands and held it tenderly. "Just like this one."

The moments fell quietly. Only the pelting rain on the roof and the moan of the wind disturbed the silence. Larry looked at Cal and smiled, then sipped his coffee. He put the cup down. "What happened to him?" he asked. "Does anyone know?"

"That's the mystery," Jonathan admitted. "Oh, some of the men said he just up and lit out of the country. Others, they said he must have lost his lamp and got himself twisted back in the tunnels." His mouth pinched together, then he added, "If that happens to a man," he glanced at Cal, "or boy, he's liable to lose his mind before he loses his life." He tapped the lamp. "If a man's in one of them deep, black holes and his lamp goes out, he nearly goes crazy screamin' for help." He looked at Cal. "If you ever get lost in the dark, don't move. Just stay put. Somebody will come and find you. If you move, you'll just lose yourself and may never be found."

The wind still whipped around the corner of the cabin and the rain fell heavy. Jonathan leaned back and listened to it for a minute. "Some nights, when the wind whips around the mountain, it whistles through those shafts. Kinda reminds me of Sweeny's singing." He cocked his head and listened. "It'll make a body wonder if he's still there — deep inside that mountain." Everyone sat silently and considered it.

Larry sighed and picked up the tin cup of coffee to take one last sip of the tepid liquid. As soon as he swallowed it, a pain struck him. The cup slipped from his fingers and struck the table, spilling its contents across the rough wooden surface. The clatter of the cup startled Cal and he jumped. His wide eyes stared at his father, then over to Jonathan.

Larry merely looked down at the overturned cup. He glanced at Jonathan. "I'm sorry," he said. His voice sounded mechanical. He swallowed hard. His throat was very dry and he was having a difficult time lifting the cup out of the pool of brown liquid. The cup slipped again and bounced on the tabletop with a hollow, metallic rattle.

Jonathan leaned forward and stared at the man. His furrowed brow and firm mouth reflected his concern. "Larry? Something wrong?"

Larry stared down at his outstretched hand. Tentatively, he reached out and touched his numbed fingers. "I-I don't know what it is," he admitted. He squeezed his right hand and pinched it. "My-my hand seems to have gone to sleep." He frowned at it. "I-I can hardly feel my own pinching." He swallowed again, then caught Cal's frightened stare. Larry smiled weakly. To reassure the boy, he scooted his chair back from the table and started to stand. Suddenly, a stabbing pain shot through his forehead and he weaved and grabbed his head.

Jonathan stood and reached for him. "Sit down," he commanded. He shoved Larry down into the chair. The old man turned to look into Cal's frightened face. "It's gonna be okay."

As he did, Larry's eyes rolled and he slumped, sliding off the chair and down to the floor at Jonathan's feet.

"Dad!" Cal screamed. He jumped up and ran around to where his father had fallen.

Jonathan grabbed the boy's arm. "Wait! Let me see."

Cal stood back, his eyes filled with tears.

Jonathan knelt close to the crumpled man and checked his breathing. Although his face was pale and his open eyes were fixed in a blind, glassy stare, he was still breathing.

Cal sobbed. "What's wrong with him?"

Jonathan didn't answer, but slipped his arm under Larry's shoulders and lifted his head and upper body. He groaned. "Come on, son, help me get him over to the bed."

Cal shoved past the big man and grabbed his dad's feet. They worked their way over to the bed and laid him on his back.

Jonathan sat on the edge of the bed and got a good grip on Larry's shoulders. He shook the man violently and shouted into his face, "Larry!" He shook him again. "Can you hear me?"

There was no response but at least Larry's eyes closed. Jonathan figured that was a good sign. The old man studied Larry's drawn complexion. It was clear that his condition was far beyond any of the miner's backwoods remedies.

Cal stood at his father's other side. He looked down at

the silent figure, then through pleading eyes stared at Jonathan.

The old man ran his tongue around the inside of his mouth and sucked air between his teeth, contemplating what he had to do. He sighed. "Somethin's mighty wrong here." He looked over at Cal. The boy's eyes were pleading with the old man. "It'll be okay," Jonathan assured him. "But listen real close. I'm going to have to go for help. I ain't no doctor and your father needs one." He put his hand out and gripped Cal's shoulder. "You stared down a grizzly, so I know you got what it takes to be a real man. But, I'm gonna have to put you to the test. I gotta leave you here to take care of your dad while I go for help." He allowed a slight smile to spread his thin lips. "You'll be okay. I'll leave Jake here with you."

Cal swallowed. His eyes brimmed with tears and he wiped them with the back of his hand. "But I don't . . ."

"Now you just listen, son!" Jonathan was suddenly very firm. "It will take me all night and then some to raise anybody. It's a long way to any help, but don't worry, I'll be back."He leaned close to Cal. "Now we faced down that old bear together, didn't we?" He tousled Cal's hair. "Well, together, we can manage this too."

Cal looked at his unmoving father as Jonathan got up to prepare for his trip. The wind had slackened some and the rain stopped. It would still be rough, especially if the rain started again and the wind strengthened.

Within a few minutes he was ready. He donned his storm slicker and fueled his lantern for the long trek down the dark mountainside. He looked at Larry one last time, checking his pulse just to be sure. It felt stronger.

Cal followed the old man to the door and helped him slip his pack on. Jonathan lit the lantern, grabbed his rifle, and opened the door. Cal followed him out onto the windy porch. Jake whined and pressed his head against the old man's leg. Jonathan looked down at the aged dog. "You stay here, old friend." He patted Jake's head. The rain began again

and a blast of wind whipped around the corner of the cabin. "You two had better get back in there where it's warm and dry." He pushed Cal into the cabin and nudged Jake in after the boy. Before he shut the door, he looked at Cal. "If he should wake up, give him something warm to drink. But don't let him get out of bed for nothing." He stared at the boy. "You hear?"

Cal nodded his head. "Yes," he muttered. He swallowed hard as he watched the old man shut the door. The wind howled, and the rain increased again. Cal pushed back the window curtain and peered out into the blackness. He could barely see the glow of the lantern in the wind-driven rain. A lump of fear welled up in his throat and he pressed his nose close to the glass and watched the lantern fade and disappear into the swirling storm.

Chapter Eleven

Rain swept the mountain path with a slick surface of boot-drenching water. Darkness became a wall that was barely penetrated by Jonathan's lantern, and the wind howled around his head.

The old man held the lantern out at arm's length, swaying it from side to side in an attempt to pierce the blackness and catch some guiding glint off the rocks that outlined the steeply descending trail. He squinted into the howling wind, then inched forward, carefully feeling out each slippery step. He fought the wind for two hours. Groping his way down the black slopes of the mountain, he followed the faint trail more by memory than by vision. The rain-soaked foliage swallowed the lantern's florid glow within a dark cloud of waving branches and driving rain.

In water-soaked boots, he edged his way down the steep pathway, which had become a torrent of cascading water. As he reached the base of the sharp incline, a jagged shaft of lightning split the sky and illuminated the side of the mountain with a bright strobe. Jonathan could see the surrounding country as if it were daylight. For an instant, the trail was clearly visible. It veered to the right and then

slithered into a thick stand of spruce.

A deafening roar immediately followed the bright flash and pushed the blackness in on him from all sides, catching the old man with its cold, wet grip. Jonathan stood motionless for a moment. Orange specks still danced in his eyes and all he could see were fading ghostly images of glistening branches and sparkling rocks. His eyes adjusted as the images disappeared.

Again, the lightning flooded the night with its brilliance, revealing the pathway. He quickly stepped forward. Pushing his way through the spruce boughs, he ducked under the protective branches of a large tree. Leaning his head back against the rough bark, he took several deep breaths in an attempt to restore his strength. His back and legs throbbed with a bone-weary ache. For several minutes he stared up blankly into the relentless pelting rain, the icy drops mingling with the salty beads of sweat on his brow, forming rivulets that coursed down the sides of his cheeks.

Once he had regained his strength, he reached under his slicker to grope for his pocket watch. He held it near the lantern and strained to see the position of the slender hands. Shaking his head, he returned the timepiece to the protection of his inner pocket, then gathered his strength and pushed through the heavy branches, stumbling on into the blackness.

The cabin creaked and groaned under the heavy wind and rain, its corrugated roof rattling complaints against the whipping gale. Cal shivered and pressed his nose against the cool windowpane. It was wet, but the boy didn't notice. He peered out into the sable-draped night. Periodically, lightning darted through the ragged clouds, casting ghostly images across the ridge top. It fluttered far down into the canyon country before the empty darkness returned with a frightening roar of thunder. Without the lightning, Cal could barely see beyond the wind-whipped porch.

He turned away from the dark, icy night to stare at the

motionless figure on the bed. "Daddy." The man didn't move. Cal watched the covers rise and fall with his father's breathing. Although the rhythm was steady, the gaunt appearance of his dad's skin frightened the boy. He swallowed and approached the bed, staring down at the death-look on his father's face.

He touched Larry's cold hand. "Dad," he whispered, squeezing the hand. "Dad?" Cal's chin quivered and his eyes brimmed with tears. He blinked them back and tried to remember Jonathan's promise to return.

A flash of lightning flooded the cabin with its brilliance. Thunder vibrated from the rock spires down through the canyon country. Cal winced as he felt the cabin floor shudder beneath him.

Jake whined nervously and jumped to his feet. Looking up at the boy he whined again.

Cal went over and squatted next to the tense dog. He stroked the long gray fur. "It's gonna be okay, Jake." He could feel the animal's tightened muscles. "Jonathan will be back soon." He wanted to do something to assure the dog, but he wasn't too sure himself. He patted Jake's head. "He promised he'd be back as soon as he could." He smiled weakly. "Just don't pay any attention to the lightning. The thunder won't hurt you." He patted the dog again.

The animal enjoyed the boy's affection and nuzzled his hand. He lay down, but kept his gaze fixed on the door.

Cal got up and went to the stove. Cold damp air penetrated the archaic structure and he wanted to warm the old place. Tentatively, he touched the fire-box handle. It was mildly warm. He twisted the lever and pulled. The door squawked as it swung on its pinned hinges. An orange glow surrounded Cal's face.

Then a gust of wind whirled across the roof of the cabin and whipped over the ridge-cap. As it struck the protruding stovepipe, its sharp down-draft shot into the stove and belched a thick cloud of soot and smoke into the room.

Cal jumped back, then glanced over his shoulder at Jake.

The dog sat up, his ears perked. The youngster waved his arms at the dark cloud, quickly grabbed a split log and tossed it into the bed of glowing embers. He kicked the door shut and secured the handle. Jake cocked his head when he heard the dull clank of the cast-iron door. Cal continued to flail at the dissipating cloud as he made his way back to the window.

Jake lay down and curled his tail around his paws. He put his muzzle down on the throw rug, but was too tense to sleep. His large, brown eyes watched the boy at the window.

Cal wiped the moisture from the pane and cupped his hands around his eyes to peer intently out into the darkness. He knew the old man was somewhere down the side of the craggy mountain, deep in timber country, being swept along through the heavy rainstorm. He pressed hard against the window and strained to see if he could catch a glimmer of Jonathan's lantern. There was nothing but blackness, dense blackness, reminding Cal of Jonathan's story. This type of thick darkness drove men insane before they lost their lives to the elements. Cal shuddered. The wind moaned and rain pelted the window in whipping gusts.

Cal turned to his unconscious father, looking for a flicker of his eyelids, a sudden change that would give the boy some hope. But there was no change. His mouth twitched and he stared at his dad, hopelessness pushing down on his young mind.

Suddenly a change came over the boy's face. He jerked around and frowned at Jake. His mind raced and a deep understanding swept through his eyes. "That's it!" he blurted, causing Jake's head to pop up and his ears to raise. The dog watched the boy closely. Cal grunted, whirled around, grabbed his coat and slipped his arms into the padded sleeves. He didn't hesitate, but headed directly to the wooden table to snatch the lantern hanging above it.

Jake jumped up, his tail wagging.

Cal pulled a chair back and got up to reach the lantern. He freed it from the hook and carefully lowered it onto the table so he could jump down.

Jake was excited by the boy's quick movements.

Cal grabbed the lantern and headed for the cabin door, Jake following. Cal looked at the old shepherd. "No, Jake, you can't go. Just stay here and keep an eye on my dad." He patted the expectant dog's head, then pulled the door open and stepped into the stormy darkness. Before he closed the door, Cal looked at his father one more time. He swallowed, then glanced at Jake. "I'll be back in a little bit," he whispered.

After Cal shut the door, he stood on the porch for a few seconds. The rain was pouring down in a diagonal sheet. Every so often, the wind whipped the drops into geometrical sprays of stinging pellets. He put his sleeve over his mouth and nose and held the lantern high as he stepped out into the squall.

The lantern bobbed from side to side as it blew in the heavy gusts. Cal moved along in the hazy glow of flickering light. He half ran along the path that led down the hill toward the mine.

Within moments he reached the fork in the trail near the base of the knoll. Veering to the left, he continued along the descending pathway until he reached the old shed. He panted as he fell against the door. With a few quick gulps of air, he straightened and forced the door open against the wind, then ducked into the tiny chapel.

The building's interior was an inky void of blackness until Cal entered. His lantern pushed the darkness back into the far corners with a warm glow casting magnified shadows on the skeletal walls. The youngster tried not to notice the dancing shapes as he moved to the place of the cross.

The wind howled outside and the rain increased.

Slowly, Cal approached the hallowed setting with as much reverence as he could muster. He stared at the rugged cross touched by the lantern's light. Carefully, he set his lantern on the bench next to the Bible.

When Cal looked back up to the cross, the lantern's glow

cast rays across it, making it stand out of the darkness in luminous relief. Somehow, it now appeared larger than it had in the daylight. His wide eyes were fixed on the cross as he knelt in front of the Bible. He folded his hands, hesitating, transfixed by the sight.

Then Cal bowed his head. "Uh, God . . ." he nearly whispered. His voice was tenuous and shy, but he continued, "I'm a friend of Jonathan's." He thought a moment. "Well, maybe you already know about my dad. He's hurt bad." Cal's mouth felt like cotton and he swallowed. "I'm not sure what to say, but I'm real worried about him. P-please, Sir, will you help my dad get well?"

Cal hesitated. For several moments he knelt silently and listened to the wind as it whistled and swirled around the outside of the shed. Finally, he lifted his eyes to the cross. He blinked a tear away and it slid down his cheek. "And, Jesus, would you check up on Jonathan and make sure that he's okay?"

After Cal made his way back to the cabin to check on his father, he sat quietly by the bedside. The storm violently assaulted Mystery Mountain, buffeting the cabin with drenching gusts throughout the rest of the night. About an hour before sunrise, the wind let up and the heavy rains softened their continual drumming on the roof.

Cal continued his watch all through the lonely hours of darkness. He broke the monotony by stoking the fire and taking great pains to check on his father every few minutes. A couple of times over the course of the night, Larry stirred, but the boy was unable to rouse him from his restless sleep. Cal simply wanted some sign that his father was on the mend, but the only response he got was fitful mumbling.

As the sky turned from deep black to dull gray, Cal slipped back to the chapel. He spread his coat across his shoulders and lay down on the high-back bench. This time, he allowed Jake to accompany him down the side of the hill and the old dog curled up near the bench and watched the boy sleep.

The dog's attention was stirred, and he raised his head to look at the fluttering flame of the lantern sitting next to the Bible. Its blackened wick wavered as it soaked up the last of the fuel.

Morning lay still as the first rays of the sun streamed over the ridges and splashed light against the scattered clouds. The storm had pushed on to the north, leaving the air clean and sweet with the aroma of damp tundra. A rich fragrance spread across the upper mountain region, easing into the chapel and tugging at the boy. He stirred, his mind drifting near the edge of awareness, but the morning's soft silence allowed him to drift away, into the echoing call of the drumming rain.

Cal fought his sleepiness, deeply aware that he had to be up and vigilant. He struggled to pull himself out of his hazy state of mind. The monotonous recall of beating rain slowly faded into a distant memory until Cal was awake. His eyes flickered and he took a deep breath. Now aware of his surroundings, he realized that the wind and rain had stopped. He stretched his sore back and squinted into the glare of the morning light. For a moment he lay on the bench rubbing his eyes with his fists. Peeking again, he scanned the walls of the shed. He stretched again, then rolled to his side and looked at Jake. "Hey, boy," he muttered.

Jake rose slowly and eyed the boy. His tail barely wagged, yet he was happy to see Cal stir and pushed his muzzle into Cal's hand. Then suddenly, his ears perked and he cocked his head.

Cal sat up as he felt the dog grow tense. "What is it, Jake?" He sat still and watched the dog. For a moment he was puzzled, then he heard something.

Somewhere in the distance a faint sound bounced through the canyon. It echoed with a throbbing beat, growing stronger. Cal stood. He could feel the slight vibration of the sound as it penetrated the old shed. It was coming closer.

The hair on Jake's neck bristled and a low growl came from his throat.

Cal patted the old dog's shoulder. "Easy, boy."

Without warning, there was a sudden blast as the sound came up over the ridge and splattered across the mountainside. Cal's eyes widened and he tossed the coat off his shoulders, heading for the door. Now he knew what was making the racket. Jake was on his heels.

As he darted out of the building and into the bright morning sunlight, he was struck by a blast of wind and his hair danced on his head. Jake barked and growled. He didn't like the sight of the helicopter whirling over them. The dark metal object was silhouetted against the glare of the sunrise, filling the sky like some giant insect. It hovered for an instant then floated sideways. Cal's face lit up and he waved with both arms when he saw Jonathan's grizzled face smiling down from the front of the craft.

The chopper dipped to one side and Jonathan waved. Quickly, the pilot lifted her up a little and headed for an open area near the cabin.

Leaping and flailing his arms, Cal started up the path toward the cabin. "Jake! It's Jonathan! Come on!"

The old dog shot by Cal, barking excitedly as he streaked up the steep trail.

Jonathan was first to emerge, quickly followed by a medic. Jake jumped and scampered around the old man like a puppy, so the old man took a moment to kneel and grab the dog, hugging him affectionately. The moment he released his hold, Jake took off, ran a large circling loop, shot by Jonathan again and was off toward the cabin.

Cal dashed up the incline, waving to the old man. His legs pumped as he cut a path straight for Jonathan. As the boy and the old man reached each other, Cal buried his head against the old man's chest. Jonathan slipped an arm around the boy. "You need your coat on, son!" he shouted. "How's your father doing?"

Cal could barely hear him above the roar of the chopper. But the man's hand against his arm felt good. He looked up into the weathered face and his chin quivered.

Jonathan swept the boy up in his arms and Cal burst into uncontrolled tears. All the tensions of the night boiled up and flooded out. Cal buried his face in Jonathan's shoulder and the old man hugged him closely. "It's okay," Jonathan assured. "It's okay. Just tell me how he did last night."

Cal sniffed and swallowed. He attempted to catch his composure as Jonathan put him down to walk at his side. He stammered, "H-he didn't w-wake up." His eyes overflowed again and he looked up at the big man. "N-not even once all night!"

Jonathan glanced at the medic and nodded. The man went on inside ahead of them. The old miner stared down at Cal, then squatted in front of him. He reached up and brushed the tear streaks from his cheeks. "It'll be all right. The doc will take care of him now." He strained desperately to hold back the feeling welling up inside him, but the tears wouldn't stay down. He looked into the youngster's fearful eyes and his vision blurred. Tears spilled down the sides of his weathered cheeks and mingled with his gray beard.

Finally, the big man stood and pulled the boy to his side, starting for the cabin door. "Come on, son. We've got to gather your stuff and give the doc a hand. They're waitin' for us in Anchorage."

Chapter Twelve

The sterile hush of the hospital's hallway was abruptly shattered when two attendants shoved a gurney into the passageway. Cal looked at the motionless form of his father lying on the rolling table. The attendants didn't hesitate, but hurried down the long corridor with Carolyn scurrying at their side.

Cal's brow furrowed and he leaned forward, stretching his neck to see if he could get a glimpse of his father under the stark-white sheets.

Jonathan gently held Cal back. He let the boy watch from the doorway until the gurney reached the far end of the hall and disappeared around a corner.

The tough old man leaned close to the boy's ear and whispered, "He's going to be all right." He gave Cal's shoulder a reassuring squeeze with the tips of his fingers. Jonathan sucked in a long, weary breath and let it out through pursed lips, then nudged Cal toward the waiting room.

As they moved down the hallway, the old man's mind raced back to the stormy hours on the side of the mountain. He sifted the file of his memory to see if he could find anything that would bring back his recall of how he had made it down the mountainside and through the torrent of the night. He shook his head and scratched at his beard.

Cal looked up at the old man as they were seated for the long wait. "Is something wrong?" he asked.

Jonathan smiled at him. "No, son. Everything's just fine. I was just thinking about how I made it through the storm and got down off old Mystery Mountain. I crossed a lot of dark, trackless wilderness." His head wagged again. "I have to say, somebody must'a been praying, 'cause God was with me."

The pair continued to talk in the waiting room while Larry was wheeled down the corridor with Carolyn rushing alongside. Her brow was wrinkled and she reached for her husband's hand.

Larry's eyes fluttered, then squinted at the overhead lights passing above him. His mind struggled with the semi-conscious cloud enveloping his perception. He felt Carolyn's hand squeeze his, but he was unable to respond. Slowly he turned his head to the side and caught her fleeting image. She seemed to be floating along the corridor with him. He closed his eyes again, faintly aware that he would be sick to his stomach if he didn't stop moving.

The gurney slowed to roll around a corner and through another set of double doors. Now the gurney was barely moving. Larry heard a man's voice. He thought it was one of the attendants talking to the other. His eyes opened again and he blinked several times trying to clear his blurred vision. Then he saw Carolyn clearly. It was she. She was there and she was holding his hand. To Larry, she was never more beautiful. He wanted to reach up and brush the furrows from her brow. With as much effort as he could gather, he worked his numb cheek muscles into a weak smile. His coated tongue pushed out to lick his lips and he forced his thoughts into whispers. "I-I'm pretty. . ."

Carolyn couldn't hear him and leaned down. She put her slender finger across his lips. "Shhh!" she cautioned. "Don't try to talk right now. Save your strength."

Larry was insistent. "I have to say it." He swallowed. "I'm good at lousing things up." His speech was slurred and he pushed aside the darkness that threatened to put him to sleep again. "I've settled on one thing."

Again, Carolyn attempted to get him to save his strength. "I'm sure the doctor doesn't want you to talk."

He closed his eyes, laboring with the mental gymnastics that added confusion to his blurred senses. His mind desperately tried to form his thoughts into intelligible patterns. "I'll never love anyone the way I love you." A tear slipped out of the corner of his eye and slid down the side of his face.

The gurney stopped. Carolyn looked up at the attendant. The young man's mouth was set. "I'm sorry, but you'll have to go back to the waiting room."

She looked down at Larry and gave his hand a final squeeze. Then she watched as they rolled the gurney into the operating room and the doors banged together, closing her out of the sterile world of surgery. As the doors swung again and settled into stillness, her mind swirled in a pool of conflicting emotions. Although she hated the feeling, she couldn't seem to help the deep, bitter resentment that swelled up in her mind. What disturbed her was the fact that Larry had succeeded again; she had run to his bidding, filled with remorse and pity. She bit her lower lip and swallowed as she continued to stare at the double doors, feeling that he had managed to maneuver her into his corner once more. Carolyn envisioned herself; as always, she had played the weak, helpless fool.

A nurse pushed through one door and looked at her. "You'll have to wait down the hall," she ordered.

Carolyn turned to mechanically walk toward the waiting room. Her mind raced and she mumbled, "Nothing's really changed." In fact, she figured that things had only become more complicated.

Her posture slumped as she ambled along the corridor,

aimless in her understanding of a future. Her lips pressed into thin lines as she gathered a stern expression and moved toward the waiting room.

Exhausted from his long and stormy trek, Jonathan had collapsed into the soft seat of the waiting room couch. His head bent back against the cushion and his mouth gapped wide while intermittent snores growled from his depths.

Cal was stretched out with his head laid on Jonathan's lap.

When Carolyn came into the room, she stopped to absorb the scene. A slight smile tugged at her mouth for a moment, then she took a chair. Settling in, she watched the old man's heavy breathing from across the room. She eyed the rugged, leathery man and wondered what strange and wonderful attraction such a bush recluse possessed, to have so quickly enchanted her boy. Cal wasn't the kind of child who took to that sort of man easily. Yet the old man had indeed made a friend of the boy.

Carolyn leaned her head back wearily and thought. It seemed just a few days ago that she had hugged a little boy and wished him well on his long-awaited adventure. Now, as she watched the pair sleeping, Cal appeared much more grown up and independent. She felt a strong remorse as the knowledge that she'd be losing him to the relentless thief of time and maturity overwhelmed her. She wished he'd remain a child. Slowly, she drifted off into exhausted sleep.

"Mrs. Sanders?"

Carolyn sat up. "Yes." She blinked and looked up into the face of Larry's surgeon. His somewhat drawn expression carried the weary marks of intense hours.

Smiling to reassure her, he sat down in the chair beside her and spoke quietly. He carried a confident air. "Your husband handled surgery very well. He's had a severe concussion and internal bleeding." The doctor lifted a hand. "Not to worry, we took care of that, and there'll be no permanent paralysis."

Carolyn barely assimilated all the doctor was saying, but she sat up straight and searched his deep blue eyes. "And?" she questioned.

The surgeon smiled. "And he's in recovery. And he should sleep through the rest of the night. And I'll look in on him in the morning." He touched the back of her hand. "In the meantime, is there anything I can do for you?"

Carolyn shook her head. "No. No thank you. I-I'm fine."

He continued in a fatherly fashion. "Well, if you would like, you can see him later tonight." He waited for a response, but she gave none. "I'll tell the nurse that you'll be in to see him. But I have to tell you, he'll be asleep." Still Carolyn didn't respond. "Sleep is the best thing for him at this juncture."

Carolyn merely nodded again and gazed across the room at Cal and Jonathan. She barely noticed the surgeon slip out of the waiting room. She rose and stood motionless for a few seconds. Her mind wouldn't accept all that had taken place and she was anxious to get her head on a pillow to find peaceful relief.

Finally, she tiptoed across the room and gently nudged Cal. "Come on, sweetheart. Time to go home."

Jonathan stirred and stared at her. He looked down at the sleeping boy in his lap. His rugged face spread into a pleasant grin and he looked back up at Carolyn. "I'll carry him," he whispered.

In the kitchen, Cal and Jonathan laced the evening meal with colorful accounts of the mining camp, Mystery Mountain and old man Sweeny. It was a fun meal for Cal, but the two adults were tense and let the boy carry most of the conversation. Cal's excitement pierced the atmosphere and charged them with a resurgence of energy.

As soon as his plate was cleared, Cal left the kitchen table and scurried upstairs. He called back to say he would return shortly with a surprise for the old man.

Jonathan sipped his coffee thoughtfully. "That's one fine

boy you got there."

Carolyn didn't comment, but kept drying the dinner dishes.

Jonathan pondered the moment. He was reluctant to speak the full breadth of his thoughts. Yet he couldn't stop what was on his mind. He sipped the dark liquid once again, then cleared his throat. "Don't normally poke my nose into other people's business, Ma'am, but your boy got me to thinkin'." The old man hesitated and swirled the coffee around in the bottom of the cup, carefully measuring his words. "I have a boy of my own, you know."

Carolyn came to life. She turned to face Jonathan. "Oh?" she responded. Her eyes narrowed. There was something in the air and she wasn't sure she liked the feel of it.

"Yup," he laughed, "and having Cal around my cabin sure stirred up a lot of memories that I'd packed in hiding long ago." He paused and gnawed at his lower lip as the thoughts become words. "I'm afraid some of those memories kinda sting." He pushed his lips out and cocked his head, looking up at Carolyn's stare. "After my wife passed on, me and my boy had a terrible fallin' out. Oh," he swirled the coffee nervously again, "the reason seemed important at the time, but now that I look back on it all, I don't suppose it amounted to a hill 'o beans." He hesitated and locked his eyes onto Carolyn's to make certain his next sentence would make its impact. "Now, I can clearly see *I'm* the real loser."

Carolyn's jaw tightened. She folded her arms across her chest and allowed the dish towel to flip over her shoulder. The feeling welling up inside her made her nostrils dilate. "What did Larry tell you about us?" Her jaw was set now.

Jonathan put his cup down and leaned back in his chair, rocking a little on the back legs. He scratched his beard and sighed. "Mostly, he said you were a fine woman and that he'd caused you considerable hurt." He detected a flash of resentment streak across her eyes and he allowed his chair to come forward as he picked up his cup again, sloshing the coffee around a bit. "Funny thing about blame," he muttered, putting the cup to one side. "It's an easy thing to shop for, but it always costs too much."

Cal clomped down the stairs and burst into the kitchen cradling a large all-band shortwave radio. He ran to the table and shoved the radio in front of Jonathan. "Here's the radio Dad promised to give you!" His excitement generated a covering for the serious conversation the old man was having with Carolyn. Cal didn't notice and continued in excited chatter. "Dad says its a real good one." He pointed to the many numbers stretched across the shiny plexiglas face. "Look! It can hear stations from all over the world!"

Jonathan grinned at the excited boy, then stroked the metal cabinet. His eyes shimmered with delight, not so much for the use of a fine radio, but for the complete abandonment of the boy. Cal always brought back the finest memories for the miner. He tousled Cal's hair. "Say, it sure is a beauty, really special. But it's a mighty expensive present."

"Yeah!" Cal agreed. "It sure is!"

Jonathan burst into laughter at Cal's unrestrained exuberance.

Carolyn blushed. "Cal!" She caught his attention with a motherly frown, then she smiled coyly at Jonathan. "We do owe you a great deal, Mister. . ." She frowned. "Ah, I'm sorry, I guess I don't know your family name."

"Oh," the old man smiled, "Jonathan will do just fine." He chuckled again and ruffled Cal's hair affectionately. The boy yawned. "Looks like it's past your bedtime, son." He took out his pocket watch and squinted at the dial. Jonathan turned the watch toward the boy. "This thing still runnin?"

Cal leaned across the table and peered at it. "Sure, it's ten 'till seven."

"Whew!" the old man exclaimed, scratching his chin whiskers. "I better be movin'." He put the watch away and scooted his chair back. "You know, it worked out real good, me being here in town when Billy Graham is up here in our neck of the woods." He stood and tucked in his shirttail. The old man's eyes lit into twinkling ovals of delight. "I never thought I'd get the chance to hear him in person. I better be gettin' over to the Sullivan Arena."

"Why, that's several miles," Carolyn said. She frowned, "That's too far for you to walk.'"

"Ha," Jonathan countered, his eyes twinkling boyishly. "Why, it's no more than a little jaunt for a mountain man."

Cal's face spread into an excited smile. "Hey, I know!" He tugged at the old man's sleeve. "We'll take you in the Blazer!" The youngster turned to his mother. "We'll take him, won't we, Mom?"

Carolyn couldn't assimilate the thought of a preaching service with thousands of milling people with the harsh realities of the day. She wanted to find something to neutralize Cal's suggestion, but nothing came to her and the moment hung too long. Carolyn forced a smile and nodded to the old miner. "Why not?" she laughed.

Chapter Thirteen

Sullivan Arena was teeming with eager people of all ages. This was Jonathan's dream of dreams. The man held the boy's hand tightly as he pressed into the crowd, opening a pathway through the bustling hallway for Cal and Carolyn.

Carolyn looked at the back of the old man's head as he continued forward. She followed in his wake, surprised that this man, so accustomed to solitude, could easily adapt to the challenge of such a throng.

Jonathan pushed on. A smile broke across his rugged features when the sound of Cliff Barrows' voice echoed in the long, gray corridor. The familiarity of the gentle baritone drew Jonathan with magnetic force. He pulled Cal along, and Carolyn rushed to keep up. The big man looked back. "They're getting ready to introduce him!" Jonathan was as excited as a little boy.

The three made their way down the long hall, around a pillar, and onto a ramp just as Dr. Graham came to the microphone.

"During this crusade, God is near," he proclaimed. His voice reverberated from one concrete pillar to another.

Jonathan caught a glimpse of him.

With his hands on his hips, Billy Graham continued, "People have prayed and people have worked. This hasn't taken place by accident. You didn't come here to see a show, or to hear a fellow by the name of Billy Graham." He paused and looked across the auditorium.

Jonathan caught one of the attendants by the arm. "We're looking for seats." He looked back to see that Carolyn was with them. "Three," he said.

"Right down there," the attendant pointed at the next aisle. "I believe there may be a few in that section."

Jonathan nodded and hurried on, with Cal and Carolyn rushing to keep up.

Billy Graham's voice boomed through the arena. "People all over the world know that we're here for this crusade and they're praying for Alaska. And in answer to their prayers, you're here and you're closer to the Kingdom of God than you'll ever be again."

The trio turned down an aisle toward the section pointed out by the attendant. Cal looked across the vast sea of people and slowly scanned row after row, jammed with people from across the main floor up to the highest levels. He squinted. The crowd seemed to merge into the arching girders of the ceiling. Thousands of pairs of eyes were fixed on the blue-fringed platform at one end of the arena.

Carolyn, too, was stunned by the enormity of the crowd. The recollection of this scene on television didn't compare to the electrifying impact of actually being among the crowd. The atmosphere was charged with a sense of expectancy and Carolyn felt her own heart stir.

"Come on, Mom," Cal called back.

The boy's excited call recaptured her attention. She followed the old man and Cal down several steps to where they had spotted three empty seats.

When Jonathan pointed to the seats, the people closed in and allowed the trio to take the three places next to the aisle.

Jonathan thanked the man who had directed the move, then they settled in.

Cal scooted back in his seat and nuzzled close to Carolyn's arm. She patted his knee and sweetly smiled at him, then glanced around Cal to see if Jonathan was comfortable. The old man was oblivious of his surroundings. The twinkle in his eye and the intent and solemn expression of his face made Carolyn smile.

"Seek the Lord while He can be found," Dr. Graham's voice vibrated through the auditorium. He hesitated and scanned the audience. "Because there will come a day when you can't find Him. He's near now. Jesus of Nazareth is passing by. He may never come this way again as far as you are concerned. If you'd been the only person in the whole world, He would have stayed on that cross just for you, because He had the ability to think of you and to see you when He was on that cross. When He said, 'My God, my God, why hast Thou forsaken me?' in that terrible moment, He was alone. And God was laying upon Him the sins of us all. Your sins were laid upon Him and the Scripture says, 'He was made to be sin for us.' You're going to walk out of here through that door," he pointed, "or that door, or that one, or this one, in a few minutes and you will have made a decision, 'Yes' or 'No,' about Christ.

"Some of you may say, 'Well, maybe I'll come back another night.'" He stopped and leaned on the lectern, his deep-set eyes penetrating the minds of certain individuals among the people. "You may not." He stood straight again. "You don't know." He glanced back at the men seated behind him on the platform, then back to the crowd. "Or, 'I'll put it off, and maybe some other occasion, when things are straightened out at home a little bit better, when I've got my life straightened out and I've got my act together, maybe I'll come to God.' You'll never get it together. And that's the reason you can't come to Christ intellectually alone. You can't think your way to God, because your mind has been affected by sin."

Carolyn watched the evangelist move from one side of the podium to the other, his words filled with concern and his heart reaching out to the crowd as if the evening's message might be his last. She sensed an unmistakable ring of truth in his words, and a deep longing for peace flowed through her. It was a feeling she hadn't had for years, and it crept into her depths like a refreshing spring, surrounding and soothing her gnawing aches. A lump stuck in her throat and her mind cleared. *Oh God*, she thought, *have I lost all sense of You? Have I moved out on my own? I've never been able to pray like mother, expecting answers like she does, but let me know that You are here, and that you are interested in me. . . in us.*

Dr. Graham's voice broke into her silent prayers. "He can free you and give you joy and the peace you long for. Come! That's the great message of the Bible. Come! All who will may come. That's the great message from the cross of Christ." He hesitated again. "Come to the cross where you can find new life and purpose and meaning. Christ can bring your whole life into focus. He can give your family the purpose it has been looking for. Everywhere I go I hear of homes, even Christian homes, with tensions and problems. Couples are separated or headed for the divorce court. Why? How could this be?" Again, he scanned the eager faces across the arena. He shook his head. "Because there are those who have tragically sidestepped God's plan for marriage. One man, one woman, growing in love for a lifetime. Then it happens. One partner says, 'I want what I want. I want it now.' The other one says, 'Me first,' and a division forms. That self-first choice can and has wounded our lives forever. One partner fails and the other feels betrayed." The evangelist raised his hand and dropped it dramatically. "That's when the marriage collapses, because the walls go up and communication stops. Then when the season changes and the winds of stress blow on such marriages, the relationship of those two, which should hold them together at those times, crumbles into ashes." He glanced down at his Bible, then back up to scan the audience. "Where does it all end?" He pointed down below the platform in front of him. "Right here. Right now. It ends with forgiveness. But you say, 'I can't find forgiveness within me.' That's true. You don't have the ability to forgive until you are forgiven. Tonight Jesus Christ stands ready to forgive you so you may walk out of this great arena with His forgiveness in you." Raising a finger, he lifted his chin and looked out over the throng. "And I can guarantee, if you come tonight truly seeking forgiveness, Christ will meet your desire and give you peace, and a future and a hope."

Carolyn was spellbound by Dr. Graham's understanding. It seemed as though he had created his message just for her.

He looked up toward the section seating the three. His hand went out. "You need Christ!" he declared. "I know that He can change your life. He'll make a new creation out of you. Christ is who you're looking for. He'll satisfy your heart, He'll forgive the past, whatever it is." Again, Billy Graham placed one hand on the lectern and pushed his coat back with the other and put his fist on his hip. His voice softened and he was instantly solemn. "God has spoken to you in these past few moments, and you know that you need to make a commitment to Him. I'm going to ask you to get up out of your seat and come and stand here." He looked out across the crowd. "And by standing here, you're saying silently, 'I open my heart to Christ. I'm willing to change my way of life through the power of Christ's Holy Spirit. I receive Him as my Lord, my Master, my Saviour, I seek forgiveness.'"

Dr. Graham stood erect and spread his arms. "Come tonight and meet Jesus Christ. You'll never be disappointed in Him." Once again he looked up toward the section where Carolyn, Cal, and Jonathan sat. "It's Him. He's who you've been looking for."

The words burned deeply into Carolyn's heart. She hardly felt the urgent pull on her arm, and it took another sharper tug by Cal to finally catch her attention.

The youngster stretched up to whisper loudly, "I want to go down." His eyes danced with excitement. "I want to thank Jesus for answering my prayer and helping Dad."

Carolyn's mind raced, and Cal's announcement barely reached her brain before the boy turned and quickly worked his way past Jonathan's knees and out into the aisle. She reached for him, but her trembling hand faltered and hung in midair. She knew she didn't really want to stop the boy. There was no reason to restrain his eager desire to give God thanks.

She found it difficult to swallow. Her throat was dry and constricted. Tears pushed through the surface and ran down her cheeks. When she dabbed the blur from her vision, she could see Cal blending in with others now filling the aisles. The boy edged down one side and skipped along happily.

Slowly, almost unintentionally, Carolyn stood and inched toward the aisle. Although it came as a sudden impulse, Carolyn knew it was far more than a burst of emotion. God had answered her prayer; He was there, and He did care about them. She now figured that if there was any purpose in life, if there was meaning to be found in the crazy patchwork of her existence, then she had to find it. And she knew this was her moment. Her knee pushed against Jonathan's leg.

The old man scrambled to get out into the aisle, barely clearing a way in time for her determined advance. She moved past him and down the ramp after Cal.

Jonathan stood in the aisle for a long moment watching Carolyn as she hurried to catch up to her son. The old miner's brow creased as he studied their descent down the long flight of stairs. The crowd blurred, and his mind whirled back across the years, echoing down twisted pathways that were at times bitter turns, seeking out another time and another boy. A tear seeped to one corner of his eye and he wiped it away. Quickly glancing around, he painfully took the first step toward the platform.

Chapter Fourteen

A steady drizzle covered the hospital parking lot with a slow, pelting sheet of cool droplets. Carolyn shivered in the night air. The lights of the hospital glistened on the rain-soaked pavement in broken mirrored images that constantly shifted and rearranged into new patterns. The young woman ran a few steps, dodged a puddle, then stopped to regain her balance and hurry on toward the entrance. She pulled her coat tightly around her and stepped up onto the sidewalk. The crisp night air brought a flush to her cheeks, but in spite of the chill, Carolyn felt a strange warmth embracing her soul.

When she reached for the heavy glass door, a portly man pushed it open and held it for her. The big man eyed her natural beauty, smiled and nodded. Carolyn barely noticed, but thanked him and hurried through the doorway, heading for the bank of elevators on the far wall.

After getting out on the third floor, she felt a strange sense of loneliness. The corridor leading toward the nurses' station was hushed and abandoned, its lights subdued. Carolyn nearly tiptoed down the hallway, approaching the open counter as quietly as she could.

A young nurse sat reading on the other side of the high counter. Carolyn eased up and peered down at her starched uniform. "Excuse me," she whispered.

The young woman was startled and slipped her hand across the page of her magazine, marking the place with her fingertips. Her confused expression was quickly masked with an air of professionalism and a cool smile. "Yes?"

"I'm Carolyn Sanders. My husband had surgery earlier today, and the doctor said that I would be able to see him tonight."

The nurse smirked, then folded the top corner of her page. She reached for a clipboard and her voice was sterile. "Who was the physician?"

Carolyn frowned slightly. "Ah, I'm sorry. I've forgotten his name."

The young woman smirked again and glanced down at the clipboard scanning the double column of names and room numbers. "Sanders?"

"Yes."

The nurse sighed. "Your husband's first name?"

"Larry."

The nurse's finger stopped, then she looked up at Carolyn, glanced at her watch and exchanged the clipboard for another one with a chart file attached to it. She flipped through several pages, finally pausing to read one. "Doctor Beckman," she muttered. With quick, professional moves, she flipped the pages back and replaced the clipboard on its hook. "I suppose a short visit will be all right, Mrs. Sanders." Leaning forward, she pointed down to her left. "Mr. Sanders is in room 312, near the end of the hall. It's on the right." She leaned back.

Carolyn nodded, turning toward 312.

The nurse called after her, "He's still sleeping and shouldn't be disturbed."

Carolyn glanced back. "I won't wake him." She tried to step as lightly as she could, but her heels tapped out a repetitive clip along the empty corridor. She attempted

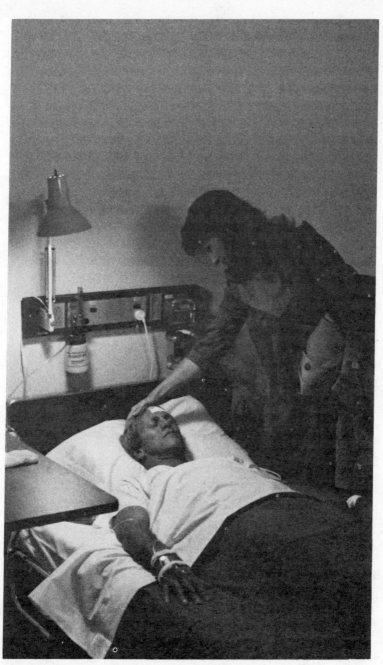

smaller steps, but that didn't help, so she lengthened her stride. The end of the hallway neared and she saw 312. Her approach slowed and anxiety created a tenuousness in her demeanor. The brass doorknob was cold and Carolyn's hand lingered before she turned it. Her eyes shifted up to stare blankly at the numbers. Finally, she sighed, resigned herself to the inevitable, and pushed the door open to step inside.

The room was dimly lit, illuminated by a single night light above Larry's bed.

Carolyn pressed the heavy door closed behind her and leaned against it. Slowly, her eyes adjusted and she studied the easy rhythm of Larry's breathing.

The monitor next to his bandaged head blinked amber lights into the subdued shadows of the room.

He moved.

Carolyn thought his eyes opened, fluttered, then closed again. She wondered if she had awakened him. "Larry?" she whispered.

He didn't move.

She inched forward with measured steps and eased over to the foot of his bed. A nervous twitch pulled at her full lips, and she hesitated, staring at his drawn features. He was sound asleep. "I know you can't hear me," she said. "You've been through a lot, I'm sure." Carolyn swallowed. "I-I thought it would be difficult coming here, talking with you." She smiled at his sleeping eyes. "I don't know why I'm even here. You've always said I had a hard time showing my true feelings." Her eyes sparkled, and she felt a deep release. "I realize you've had to pry my emotions out of me." She shook her head. "But you have to understand, and maybe someday when we can talk about this, you will. I felt like I was offering my report card." A tear spilled over her soft cheek. "It seemed that everything I did just couldn't make the grade. And I never wanted my life to be just patched-up compromises."

Larry moaned. His regulated breathing hesitated, and the monitor's amber lights broke their rhythm, then he settled again and they were back in sequence.

Carolyn watched him. Her eyes softened as a deep peace melted over her and released the knot in her throat. She swallowed easily and her chin quivered. Another tear slipped down her cheek as she made her way around the end of the bed and gently took her husband's hand. It was warm and limp. She pulled it up to her lips and kissed his fingers. The tears formed into rivulets that flowed into convulsive sobs. "I-I'm so sorry," she whispered. "I can forgive you now." The amber lights merged into geometric splashes in her dark eyes. "I can hardly wait to tell you. Something wonderful has happened tonight. I have hope...for us."

The long hours of arctic summer were past and the tundra on the upper slopes of the mountain aged to a brilliant patchwork of yellows, browns and reds. The rich hues streaked down the steep tufted slopes, mingling as they spilled between the rocky crags and splashed across the rolling knolls of Mystery Mountain.

At the base of the mountain, the birch and aspen forests were already sprinkled with the first marks of yellow and gold, and the pungent scent of highbush cranberries lay heavy in the foliage along the river's edge.

Jonathan stared through the haze of the cabin window, carefully measuring each familiar landmark of the canyon country. A satisfied smile stretched across his face as he watched the sun cast lengthening shadows down into the lower flats. The old man frowned and rubbed his sleeve on the hazy pane. He glanced at his dog. "Gonna have to scrub this window someday, Jake." He cocked his head, rubbing his whiskers. "It don't seem to let in enough light anymore."

Jake was happy that Jonathan was back and the old shepherd swished his tail as he looked up at the rugged miner.

Jonathan shuffled across the room, pausing at the bookshelf where the new shortwave receiver was proudly displayed. He studied it gently. A distant look swept across his graying eyes. He sighed and looked down at his old companion. "You remember Ethan, don't you, Jake?" The dog didn't respond and Jonathan's eyes widened into unfocused reminiscence. He continued muttering to the silent animal, "You and Ethan used to spend your days tailing rabbits. 'Course, you were just a pup then." He blinked, then smiled at Jake. "It's been a long time now." He wagged his large head. "Yup, a long time for both of us."

The moment of decision hung in the air. Then Jonathan turned back to the aged black photo album and took it down. Cradling it in his arms, he shuffled to the table and fumbled through the tattered book. He stopped at every picture, as though each separate page loosed a score of pent up memories. Silently, he studied the parade of faded photographs.

When he was little more than half way through the pages, he laid the album aside, scooted his chair back and stood. After a brief hesitation, Jonathan stepped back over to the shelving and reached up to the top shelf. He stretched and reached as high as he could, rummaging around with his hand. Finally, he felt a small tin box, clutched it, and brought it down. He dusted the lid with a quick puff of breath. Then, hooking his fingernails under its curled rim, he pried the box open. The old man stared at the envelopes and letters inside. He muttered as he shuffled through the yellowed papers. Finally, he withdrew a single crumpled envelope and held it out, squinting, trying to read the return address.

"Ha," he grunted, "this address is probably older than the hills." Absently, he set the tin box on the shelf next to the radio. Then, gathering a pencil and small spiral notebook, he headed for the wooden desk.

Jake followed the old man back to the dark recesses of the cabin. He watched as Jonathan lit a lantern and put it on the desk.

The old miner glanced down at the dog. "Letter writin's never been my strong suit, Jake." He smirked. "But you can't

tell other folks to mend their fences if you don't intend on carin' for your own."

Jake cocked his head and watched with growing curiosity as the old man tore a sheet from the pad and placed it on the table, smoothing it with several careful strokes.

Jonathan pulled his chair up and got himself situated, ready to write. He stared at the blank paper and tapped his fingers on the desk top. For several minutes he sat in the silence of the cabin, his eyes fixed on the off-white sheet. With a sigh of resignation, he pulled the paper in close and began his letter. He mouthed each word as he wrote. "Dear Son. Now don't faint dead away, not till you hear me out. . . ."

Outside the musty windows, the mining camp stood stark and lonely against the mountainside, its forsaken buildings bathed in the ruddy glow of the fading light. The camp had seen many sunsets over the passing years and would no doubt see more. But if the coming winter was harsh, some of the weathered buildings would surely crumble under their heavy mantles of snow. The ensuing summer winds would scatter the ridge with broken lumber and tangled tin. And bit by bit, Mystery Mountain would reclaim her solitude.

Perhaps other strangers would pass that way before the old man was gone, and there was always a good chance that Larry and Cal would be back within a summer or two.

One thing, for sure, would grab their attention. Along the pathway, leading up to the twisted buildings, they'd spot the sign that once refused to welcome strangers. The former words would be crossed out and painted over in bright yellow, "Visitors Welcome."

Jesus said that the Spirit of God moves over the world like the wind, touching whom He will. Reading this story, have you sensed God's Spirit calling you? What Carolyn experienced that night in Sullivan Arena is what the Bible calls being "born from above." She didn't have it all worked out the instant she went forward, but she knew that she wanted to change and she asked God to touch her life. That's what the Bible calls "repentance." Jesus said, "I am the Way, the Truth, and the Life."

I accepted that fact one day by faith and it changed my life in ways I never dreamed possible. None of us deserve salvation. It is God's free gift to those who believe. It doesn't matter what your situation is; only you and the Lord know for sure. The Bible says that He reads all hearts and that He stands ready to forgive you and give you peace and eternal life through his Son.

That's why Jesus Christ came to earth, and that's why I can ask you to make this vital decision for Christ. We're all so quick to try the world's way, and over the years we come up empty. Let God show you His way. You'll never be disappointed in Christ. Come just as you are. You may never have another moment quite like this. God bless you.

Billy Graham